PRACTICAL GUIDE TO *B*ETTER ENGLISH

Level 1

AGS®
American Guidance Service, Inc.
Circle Pines, Minnesota 55014-1796
1-800-328-2560

A NOTE TO STUDENTS

The *Practical Guide to Better English* teaches grammar, usage, mechanics, and writing skills. It is designed to help you become familiar with important elements of the English language and develop the written communication skills needed in school and in the workplace.

Completing the Lessons

Every lesson in this program is written so that you can complete it on your own. You can do this by following these steps:

1. Take a First Look

Read the lesson title. Ask yourself what you already know about this skill. If the title is "Punctuating Sentences," you might ask yourself: *What punctuation marks have I already learned about? Which of these marks are used at the end of a sentence?*

2. Learn the Rules

Look at the Handbook Guide numbers listed in the gray box at the beginning of the lesson. If there is a rule statement in the box, read it. Then find the numbered Guides in the Handbook, which starts on page 113. Read the rules and do the practice exercises. Check your answers by looking at the correct answers at the end of the numbered Guide or set of Guides. Then go back to the lesson page.

3. Think About the Topic

Scan the exercise sentences to find out what the topic is. Ask yourself: *What do I already know about this subject?* If you're working with a partner or group, share some facts about the topic. Reviewing what you already know can help you get more out of what you read.

4. Complete the Lesson

Many lessons have two parts. Read the directions for the first part and think about what you're being asked to do. Ask for help if you don't understand the directions. Then complete the exercise. Use the Handbook Guide to help you if you are uncertain about an answer. Then follow the same steps for Part II. Some lessons have a vocabulary activity at the bottom of the page. If there is a vocabulary activity, complete it last.

5. Check Your Answers

With your group or class, identify the correct answer for each item. If you have an Answer Key, check your work yourself. The Perfect Score for each lesson is given at the top of the page. Count your correct answers and write your score in the blank at the top of the page. Then record your score on the chart on page 160.

6. Sum It Up

Think about what you learned in the lesson. You might want to write the Handbook Guide rule used in the lesson in your own words. Think about how you can use this skill when you write or speak.

Reviewing What You've Learned

The last lesson in every unit gives you a chance to review the skills in that unit. The unit review lesson is not a test. It's there to help you recall what you've learned and put that new knowledge to work. The Handbook Guides are listed with each item, so you can check a rule if you need to before you complete the item.

Printed in the United States of America
ISBN 0-7854-1788-5
Product Number 93070
A 0 9 8 7 6 5 4 3

CONTENTS

UNIT I

Lesson 1   Writing Names   5

Lesson 2   Writing Titles Before Names and Initials of Names   6

Lesson 3   Using Capital Letters   7

Lesson 4   Recognizing Sentences   8

Lesson 5   Using Capital Letters   9

Lesson 6   Punctuating Sentences   10

Lesson 7   Punctuating Three Kinds of Sentences   11

Lesson 8   Using *Is* and *Are*   12

Lesson 9   Using *Was* and *Were*   13

Lesson 10   Writing Three Kinds of Sentences   14

Lesson 11   Unit I Review   16

UNIT II

Lesson 12   Reviewing Sentences   17

Lesson 13   Using *There Is* and *There Are*   18

Lesson 14   Writing the Names of Days of the Week   19

Lesson 15   Writing the Names of Months of the Year   20

Lesson 16   Writing the Names of Holidays, Special Days, and Seasons   21

Lesson 17   Capitalization   22

Lesson 18   Using *There Was* and *There Were*   23

Lesson 19   Writing Dates   24

Lesson 20   Choosing Standard Forms   25

Lesson 21   Writing Sentences Using the First-Person Voice   26

Lesson 22   Unit II Review   28

UNIT III

Lesson 23   Writing Abbreviations   29

Lesson 24   Writing Contractions   30

Lesson 25   Using Contractions   31

Lesson 26   Using *Their*, *There*, and *They're*   32

Lesson 27   Using *May* and *Can*   33

Lesson 28   Using *A* and *An*   34

Lesson 29   Writing Titles   35

Lesson 30   Punctuation and Capitalization   36

Lesson 31   Choosing Standard Forms   37

Lesson 32   Writing Sentences That Compare   38

Lesson 33   Unit III Review   40

UNIT IV

Lesson 34   Using Commas   41

Lesson 35   Using Troublesome Words   42

Lesson 36   Learning about Friendly Letters   43

Lesson 37   Writing a Friendly Letter   44

Lesson 38   Writing Envelope Addresses   45

Lesson 39   Using *Saw* and *Seen*   46

Lesson 40   Using *Did* and *Done*   47

Lesson 41   Punctuation and Capitalization   48

Lesson 42   Choosing Standard Forms   49

Lesson 43   Using the Writing Process to Write a Science Report   50

Lesson 44   Unit IV Review   52

UNIT V

Lesson 45   Punctuating Direct Quotations   53

Lesson 46   Using Quotation Marks   54

Lesson 47   Writing Singular and Plural Forms of Words   55

Lesson 48   Writing Singular and Plural Words   56

Lesson 49   Using *Went* and *Gone*   57

Lesson 50   Using *Flew* and *Flown*   58

Lesson 51   Writing Words in Alphabetical Order   59

Lesson 52   Writing More Words in Alphabetical Order   60

Lesson 53   Choosing Standard Forms   61

Lesson 54   Writing a Summary   62

Lesson 55   Unit V Review   64

UNIT VI

Lesson 56   Dividing Words   65

Lesson 57   Sticking to the Paragraph Topic   66

Lesson 58   Combining Sentences   67

Lesson 59   Avoiding Too Many *Ands*   68

Lesson 60	Finding Synonyms	69
Lesson 61	Using Synonyms	70
Lesson 62	Choosing Homophones	71
Lesson 63	Finding Antonyms	72
Lesson 64	Choosing Standard Forms	73
Lesson 65	Writing a Descriptive Paragraph	74
Lesson 66	Unit VI Review	76

UNIT VII

Lesson 67	Using *Has* and *Have*	77
Lesson 68	Learning to Use Troublesome Contractions	78
Lesson 69	Using Contractions	79
Lesson 70	Using *I* and *Me*	80
Lesson 71	Using *Come* and *Came*	81
Lesson 72	Using *Took* and *Taken*	82
Lesson 73	Learning to Use Homophones	83
Lesson 74	Learning to Use Commas	84
Lesson 75	Choosing Verb Forms	85
Lesson 76	Writing a Persuasive Paragraph	86
Lesson 77	Unit VII Review	88

UNIT VIII

Lesson 78	Capitalization	89
Lesson 79	Punctuation	90
Lesson 80	Using *We* and *Us*	91
Lesson 81	Forming Possessives	92
Lesson 82	Using Negatives	93
Lesson 83	Avoiding Unnecessary Words	94
Lesson 84	Spelling Synonyms	95
Lesson 85	Using *Himself* and *Themselves*	96
Lesson 86	Choosing Standard Forms	97
Lesson 87	Using the Writing Process to Write a Personal Narrative	98
Lesson 88	Unit VIII Review	100

UNIT IX

Lesson 89	Reviewing Sentences	101
Lesson 90	Reviewing Standard Forms	102
Lesson 91	Reviewing More Standard Forms	103
Lesson 92	Reviewing Punctuation and Capitalization	104
Lesson 93	Reviewing Synonyms and Antonyms	105
Lesson 94	Reviewing Singular and Plural Words	106
Lesson 95	Reviewing Possessives and Contractions	107
Lesson 96	Reviewing Uses of a Dictionary	108
Lesson 97	Reviewing Standard Forms	109
Lesson 98	Unit IX Review	110

THE HANDBOOK   113

Capitalization	114
Capitalization with Punctuation	117
Other Uses of Commas	123
Contractions	126
Singular and Plural Forms of Nouns	127
Possessive Forms of Nouns	128
Principal Parts of Verbs	129
The Sentence	130
The Paragraph	133
Speaking and Listening	135
The Report	137
The Story	138
The Letter	139
Troublesome Words	143
Word Study	148
The Dictionary	153
Handbook Index	158
Score Chart	160

Name_____   Perfect Score 48   My Score _____

LESSON 1
Writing Names

Handbook Guides 1b, 1f
Begin the name of a person, a pet, a place, or an organization with a capital letter.

PART 1   In the following sentences, underline the uncapitalized words that should begin with a capital letter. (Score: 38)

Example:

Pets in santa cruz are safer with kat albrecht around!

1. kat albrecht is a police officer for the university of california at santa cruz.

2. In her spare time she runs the pet pursuit agency.

3. Her three partners, rachel, chase, and A. J., are all dogs!

4. They sniff out lost pets in communities near monterey bay.

5. albrecht may be a pet detective, but she's not goofy like ace ventura.

6. This expert even sends hair samples to a lab in hayward, california.

7. One of albrecht's happy clients is catherine murray.

8. This aptos high school teacher had lost her cat tony.

9. albrecht brought rachel and searched the area.

10. Then murray told her that the roof had just been repaired.

11. albrecht and rachel found tony hiding in the repair van.

12. albrecht hopes to start a new agency to help pet owners across the united states.

13. The national center for missing pets will be its name.

PART II   In the blank spaces, write names for the following items. (Score: 10)

Examples: a cat   *Smudge*   a company   *Sunrise Market*

14. a city _____   19. a school _____

15. a country _____   20. a park _____

16. a person _____   21. a lake _____

17. a river _____   22. a club _____

18. a state _____   23. a dog _____

Name _____   Perfect Score 36   My Score _____

LESSON 2
Writing Titles Before Names and Initials of Names

Handbook Guides 1b, 1c, 1d, 1f, 2, 3

Use a capital letter to begin a title before a person's name. Place a period after the title if it is abbreviated.

Use a capital letter to write the initial of a name. Place a period after the initial.

PART I   Rewrite the following paragraph. Use capital letters and periods where they are needed. (Score: 33)

Have you heard of a powder named super slurper? It was developed by dr william doane of the united states department of agriculture. He was helped by dr george fanta, dr ed bagley, and ms m o weaver. super slurper is made from cornstarch. It is a very thirsty powder. One pound of it can soak up a thousand pounds of water. dr doane's discovery is used in fuel filters, bandages, and ice packs. Perhaps super slurper may one day be used to dry out flooded basements.

_____

_____

_____

_____

_____

_____

_____

_____

_____

_____

_____

PART II   Write a title and name for each of the following. Use initials in place of first and middle names. (Score: 3)

Example: a general   _General H. N. Schwarzkopf_

1.   a doctor _____

2.   a senator _____

3.   an actress _____

LESSON 3
Using Capital Letters

PART I   Write a sentence with each name below. Use a title of respect with each person's name. (Score: 20—2 for each sentence)

Example:

lincoln center   *They took a trip to Lincoln Center.*

1.   kansas city _____

2.   taneytown road _____

3.   coney island _____

4.   nagy's cleaners _____

5.   wabash river _____

6.   jacobs field _____

7.   theodore roosevelt _____

8.   lisa leslie _____

9.   grant hill _____

10. coretta scott king _____

PART II   Write sentences with the names of seven people you know. Use initials in place of first and middle names. (Score: 14—2 for each sentence)

11. _____

12. _____

13. _____

14. _____

15. _____

16. _____

17. _____

Optional Exercise: Find the names of five people in a newspaper. Write sentences with the names. Use titles and use initials instead of first and middle names.

Name _____   Perfect Score 16   My Score_____

LESSON 4
Recognizing Sentences

Handbook Guide 17a

A sentence is a group of related words that expresses a complete thought.

Write the word *yes* before each group of words that is a sentence. Write the word *no* before each group that needs something else to complete the thought. (Score: 16)

Examples:

_____*yes*_____   Have you lived in Hawaii very long?

_____*yes*_____   The weather in most parts of Hawaii is agreeable all year.

_____*no*_____   Sitting on the beach because the sun is so warm.

The Valley Island

_____ 1. How cold is the weather in January in your part of the country?

_____ 2. Most January days warm and pleasant on Maui.

_____ 3. Maui is the second largest island in Hawaii.

_____ 4. Maui is known as the Valley Island.

_____ 5. Many green valleys on the slopes of Maui's two volcanoes.

_____ 6. People have come from many lands to live on Maui.

_____ 7. Polynesians rowing huge canoes to the shores of Maui long ago.

_____ 8. These Polynesian settlers brought many useful plants to Hawaii.

_____ 9. Planted bananas, coconuts, taro, sweet potatoes, and sugarcane.

_____ 10. Pineapples, which were brought from South America much later.

_____ 11. Many people came to help raise these crops.

_____ 12. People from Europe, Asia, and other Pacific islands.

_____ 13. American missionaries came to Maui early in the nineteenth century.

_____ 14. The port of Lahaina, a whaling village.

_____ 15. Some of the whalers were rowdy folk.

_____ 16. Maui's history is as colorful as its tropical flowers.

Name_____ Perfect Score 78 My Score _____

UNIT
I

LESSON 5
Using Capital Letters

Handbook Guides 1a, 1b, 1e, 1f, 2, 3, 17b

Use a capital letter to begin the first word of a sentence. Write the word *I* with a capital letter.

PART I Underline each word, initial, or abbreviation that should begin with a capital letter. Place periods where they are needed. (Score: 63)

Example:

the story i will tell you is true.

1. daniel james was the youngest of seventeen children.

2. his family lived in pensacola, florida.

3. the father of daniel james was a coal-cart pusher.

4. daniel's mother was named lillie anna james.

5. according to daniel, education was like a religion to mrs james.

6. she had her children read aloud to her almost every night.

7. the children also put on plays for mr and mrs james.

8. daniel was often called by the nickname chappie.

9. in 1937 chappie received a football scholarship to tuskegee institute in alabama.

10. however, chappie did not get along well with some students and teachers.

11. he got into some fights and was thrown out of tuskegee institute.

12. then chappie met mr b o davis, who helped him settle down.

13. chappie went back to tuskegee institute and finished his studies.

14. early in World War II chappie learned to fly a plane.

15. chappie james was later an ace flier in korea and vietnam.

16. in the Air Force he became gen. daniel "chappie" james, the first African American four-star general.

17. now do you know why i admire chappie james?

PART II Write three sentences about people you admire. Use the word *I* in each sentence. (Score: 15—5 for each sentence)

18. _____

19. _____

20. _____

LESSON 6
Punctuating Sentences

Place the appropriate mark at the end of each sentence below. (Score: 20)

Examples:

Is Alice our pitcher? *(asking sentence)*

Alice is our pitcher. *(telling sentence)*

Stickball

1.   Have you ever played stickball

2.   Many young people in New York City have played this game

3.   A stick is used as a bat

4.   Is it easy to hit a ball with a thin stick

5.   This game is usually played with a soft rubber ball

6.   The game should be played on a street with no traffic

7.   Why is the person at bat standing near that manhole cover

8.   The cover is home plate

9.   The pitcher must throw a pitch that bounces once

10.   Do you know what the strike zone is

11.   Was that pitch really a ball

12.   It was below the batter's knees

13.   Wasn't it really above the knees and over the plate

14.   Is that Charlene's team in the field

15.   Buddy is the catcher, Charlene is the pitcher, and Brenda is the infielder

16.   Who is the outfielder

17.   Alicia hit a long foul fly ball onto Mrs. DiNardo's porch

18.   In this game the ball must land on the street to be a fair ball

19.   Can you become a good baseball player by playing stickball

20.   Which big league stars played stickball when they were young

LESSON 7
Punctuating Three Kinds of Sentences

> **Handbook Guides 17c, 17d, 17e**
>
> **Place a period at the end of a telling sentence. Place a question mark at the end of an asking sentence. Place an exclamation point at the end of an exclamatory sentence.**

Place the appropriate punctuation mark at the end of each of the following sentences. If the sentence is a telling sentence, write *T* in the blank before the sentence; if it is an asking sentence, write *A*; and if it is an exclamatory sentence, write *E*. (Score: 24)

Examples:

___*T*___   The moose is a member of the deer family.

___*A*___   Is that a moose standing near those birch trees?

___*E*___   Look at the size of that animal!

The Mighty Moose

_____ 1.   The moose is the largest deer in the world

_____ 2.   Can a moose weigh as much as a small car

_____ 3.   I wouldn't want either one to sit on me

_____ 4.   What a clumsy-looking animal that is

_____ 5.   What was that noise

_____ 6.   Look at that moose run

_____ 7.   Many moose can run faster than 45 mph

_____ 8.   Twigs are a favorite food of moose

_____ 9.   Why is that moose standing in the middle of the lake

_____ 10. It's keeping cool and avoiding the insects

_____ 11. Are moose always shy and peaceful

_____ 12. An angry moose can sometimes beat a grizzly bear in a fight

Odd Word Out _____

Circle the word in this list that does not belong with the others. Name a category that would fit the three uncircled words. Then name a category for the word you circled.

omnivore   matador   herbivore   carnivore

Name_____   Perfect Score 17   My Score _____

LESSON 8
Using Is *and* Are

Handbook Guide 28a

Use *is* **when speaking of one person or thing. Use** *are* **when speaking of more than one person or thing.**

Fill each blank with *is* or *are*. (Score: 17)

Examples:

A desert _____*is*_____ not a wasteland.

Some plants and animals _____*are*_____ well suited for desert life.

1. A desert _____ a region that gets very little rain.

2. Desert soil _____ very dry.

3. Desert plants _____ spaced far apart because there is very little water to share.

4. Mesquite trees _____ able to grow well in the desert because of their deep roots.

5. After rain falls, a desert _____ a colorful sight.

6. Many plants _____ covered with flowers.

7. For many desert plants, the life cycle _____ very short.

8. The rain showers _____ the signal for plants to sprout, flower, and then drop seeds and die.

9. Lizards, tortoises, and kangaroo rats _____ all desert dwellers.

10. Kangaroo rats _____ found in deserts in Mexico and the southwestern United States.

11. This rat _____ a close relative of the pocket mouse.

12. Like the mouse, it _____ able to live on moisture from its food.

13. The kangaroo rat _____ able to live where there are no creeks or ponds.

14. During the daytime, the rat _____ cool and safe in its den under the ground.

15. At night it _____ busy filling its cheeks with food.

16. Kangaroo rats _____ great jumpers.

17. That _____ how they got their name.

LESSON 9
Using Was *and* Were

> **Handbook Guide 28**
> Use *was* when speaking of only one person or thing. Use *were* when speaking of more than one person or thing. Always use *were* with *you*.

Fill each blank with *was* or *were*. (Score: 16)

1. In the early 1800s, St. Louis _____ a small town.

2. It _____ the spot where Lewis and Clark began and ended their famous expedition.

3. Soon many other Easterners _____ passing through this gateway city.

4. They _____ on their way to Oregon or California.

5. St. Louis _____ a good place to buy supplies.

6. Wagons, mules, and saddles _____ available there.

7. Stores _____ well stocked with dried beans, dried bread, and crackers.

8. The city _____ also an important river port in those days.

9. Its docks _____ crowded with barges and riverboats.

10. By 1904 it _____ the fourth largest city in the United States.

11. In that year a huge world's fair _____ held in St. Louis.

12. Twenty million people _____ entertained by shows, displays, and rides.

13. Ice cream cones _____ invented at the fair.

14. The inventors of this treat _____ Ernest Hamwi and Arnold Fornachou.

15. Hamburgers in buns _____ also introduced to many people at the fair.

16. These foods _____ both instant hits because they let people walk and eat at the same time!

Word Whiz _____

Use the clues on the left to help you complete the words on the right. Use a dictionary for spelling help.

settler   p __ __ __ e   e   r

place where unsettled land begins   f   r __ __ __ __ i   e   r

to guide   s __ e   e   r

Name_____

LESSON 10
Writing Three Kinds of Sentences

Think About Sentences

Handbook Guides 1a–f, 17a–e

A telling sentence is a statement. It ends with a period.

An asking sentence asks a question. It ends with a question mark.

An exclamatory sentence shows strong feeling. It ends with an exclamation point.

You use different kinds of sentences for different reasons when you speak and write. Read the items below. Circle the answers that tell when each type of sentence should be used. There are two correct answers for each item.

1. Use a telling sentence if you need to _____.

   a. find out the score of a baseball game
   b. describe what a place looks like
   c. give information about a science topic
   d. warn someone about a charging bull

2. Use an asking sentence if you need to _____.

   a. find out when the bus will arrive
   b. get directions to a place
   c. describe a person you know well
   d. give a recipe to a friend

3. You might use an exclamatory sentence if you _____.

   a. suddenly see a huge snake
   b. want to know the time
   c. give directions to the park
   d. dive into an icy lake

Write Sentences

Read each statement below. Then write the correct kind of sentence in response. Remember to capitalize the first word of each sentence, and to use the correct end marks.

Example: You need to find out what time the basketball game begins.

   *What time does the basketball game begin?*_____

4. You need to find out what time the train leaves for Detroit.

   _____

   _____

5. A black widow spider has just landed on your shoulder.

   _____

   _____

6. You must explain why you were late for karate class.

_____

_____

7. You want to know whether wolves, coyotes, and dogs are related.

_____

_____

8. You are curious about whether or not your friends were at a certain party.

_____

_____

9. You just realized that you missed the last bus, and now you have to walk home in the rain.

_____

_____

10. You need to inform a friend that you'll meet him at 8:00 P.M.

_____

_____

Revise Sentences

There is something wrong with each group of words below. Some are not really sentences because they are missing important words. Others have mistakes in capitalization and punctuation. Rewrite each sentence so it is correct and complete.

11. dr briggs lives in colorado.

_____

12. was trudy born in denver or in boulder!

_____

13. What a huge fish that is

_____

14. swimming in a murky pond

_____

15. mrs g b macIntire my violin teacher

_____

Name_____   Perfect Score 28   My Score _____

LESSON 11
Unit 1 Review

1. Write the full names of two of your friends. Then rewrite these names, using your friends' initials instead of the given names. Use periods where needed. (Score: 4)   **Handbook Guides 1b, 1d, 2**

    _____   _____

    _____   _____

2. Write the names of four towns or cities in your state. (Score: 4)   **Handbook Guide 1f**

    _____   _____

    _____   _____

3. Write three full names, using a different title before each. (Score: 3)   **Handbook Guides 1b, 1c, 3**

    _____

    _____

    _____

4. Rewrite these sentences, using capital letters and punctuation where needed. (Score: 13)   **Handbook Guides 1b–d, 2, 3, 17b–d**

    where did i meet mrs d s elarmo _____

    _____

    the name of our new bulldog is smiley _____

    _____

5. Write two asking sentences. Use the word *is* in the first one and the word *are* in the second one. (Score: 2)   **Handbook Guides 17d, 28**

    _____

    _____

6. Write two telling sentences. Use *was* in the first one and *were* in the second. (Score: 2)   **Handbook Guides 17c, 28**

    _____

    _____

LESSON 12
Reviewing Sentences

Handbook Guides 1a, 17b–e

Place the appropriate punctuation mark after each of the following sentences. Underline each uncapitalized word that should begin with a capital letter. If the sentence is a telling sentence, write *T* in the blank space before the sentence. If it is an asking sentence, write *A*. If it is an exclamatory sentence, write *E*. (Score: 45)

Examples:

_____*T*_____   cats have been friends to people for four thousand years.

_____*A*_____   have you seen old Egyptian paintings of cats?

_____*E*_____   how beautiful some of the cats are!

Rich Cat, Poor Cat

_____   1.   cats were treated with great respect in ancient Egypt

_____   2.   there were even special cemeteries for cats

_____   3.   what a strange idea this is to us

_____   4.   what happened to people who killed cats

_____   5.   a person who killed a cat was put to death at once

_____   6.   times were hard for cats in the Middle Ages

_____   7.   how people feared cats then

_____   8.   were cats believed to be evil

_____   9.   it was thought that cats caused hurricanes and sickness

_____   10.   trouble came to anyone who owned a black cat

_____   11.   were people frightened when a cat arched its back

_____   12.   get that cat away from me

_____   13.   this cat has very long back legs and no tail at all

_____   14.   haven't you ever seen a Manx cat before

_____   15.   this cat attacks rats, mice, and even snakes

Optional Exercise: Write three sentences that ask questions about cats and three sentences that answer the questions.

Name_____   Perfect Score 18   My Score _____

LESSON 13
Using There Is *and* There Are

Handbook Guide 28c

Use *there is* or *is there* when speaking of one person or thing. Use *there are* or *are there* when speaking of more than one person or thing.

Fill each blank with *there is*, *there are*, *is there*, or *are there*. (Score: 18)

Wonders Beneath the Waves

1. _____ many strange sights at the bottom of the sea.

2. _____ a boat with a glass bottom.

3. In it _____ eight people who want to see the bottom of the ocean.

4. _____ many odd creatures to be seen.

5. _____ any dangerous sharks in this area?

6. Far to the right _____ a great wall of coral.

7. _____ several large rays with whiplike tails.

8. _____ a blue-green parrotfish near the coral.

9. _____ other fish that have a jaw shaped like a parrot's beak?

10. _____ many fish hiding among the rocks.

11. _____ an octopus in sight?

12. _____ cups on the octopus's long arms.

13. _____ two green eyes in the center of its forehead.

14. _____ a tiny yellow and blue fish near the octopus.

15. _____ a huge kelp forest not too far away.

16. _____ a diver with a mask and an air tank.

17. _____ air bubbles rising toward the surface.

18. On all sides of us _____ beautifully colored fish.

Find the Goof _____

Rewrite the sentence in which the boldfaced word is used incorrectly. Replace the boldfaced word with the word that should be there.

Is there an **antidote** for a jellyfish sting?
The diver told us an amusing **antidote**.

LESSON 14
Writing the Names of Days of the Week

> **Handbook Guides 1b, 1h, 4, 17b–e**
>
> **Begin the name of each day of the week or its abbreviation with a capital letter. Place a period after each abbreviation.**

PART I   In the blank space opposite, rewrite each word as it should be written. (Score: 7)

1. friday _____
2. tuesday _____
3. sunday _____
4. wednesday _____

5. monday _____
6. saturday _____
7. thursday _____

PART II   In the blank space opposite, write the abbreviation for each word. (Score: 7)

8. sunday _____
9. tuesday _____
10. saturday _____
11. thursday _____

12. monday _____
13. wednesday _____
14. friday _____

PART III   In the following sentences, place punctuation marks where they are needed. Draw a line under each word that should begin with a capital letter. (Score: 34)

15. helen was badly burned last thursday in an apartment fire

16. on friday she was flown to a burn treatment center at a distant hospital

17. doctors gave helen large amounts of fluids all day friday

18. on saturday helen was put into a tub of warm water

19. was she bathed again on sunday morning

20. by monday afternoon the doctors had finished planning her treatment

21. helen's first operation was on tuesday

22. what terrible pain helen felt on wednesday

23. did the doctors talk about skin grafts for her on thursday

24. a doctor told helen friday night that she was doing much better than expected

Optional Exercise: Imagine you are helping care for someone who has been badly hurt. Tell one thing you did for that person on each day of the week. Be sure to write each day of the week as it should be written.

Name_____   Perfect Score 67   My Score _____

LESSON 15
Writing the Names
of Months of the Year

> **Handbook Guides 1a, 1b, 1h, 4, 5, 17b–d**
>
> **Begin the name of each month of the year or its abbreviation with a capital letter. Place a period after each abbreviation.**

PART I   In the blank space opposite, rewrite each word as it should be written. (Score: 12)

1. january _____   7. july _____

2. february _____   8. august _____

3. march _____   9. september _____

4. april _____   10. october _____

5. may _____   11. november _____

6. june _____   12. december _____

PART II   In the blank space opposite, rewrite each abbreviation as it should be written. (Score: 9)

13. jan _____   16. apr _____   19. oct _____

14. feb _____   17. aug _____   20. nov _____

15. mar _____   18. sept _____   21. dec _____

PART III   In the following sentences, place punctuation marks where they are needed. Draw a line under each uncapitalized word that should begin with a capital letter. (Score: 46)

22. christopher columbus first landed in the Americas on october 12, 1492

23. the first Thanksgiving Day feast was held in october of 1621

24. the Boston Tea Party happened in december of 1773

25. in april 1775, paul revere made his famous midnight ride

26. what happened during the first week of july in 1776

27. we remember the birthdays of george washington and abraham lincoln each february

28. since 1789 Americans have celebrated Thanksgiving Day each november

29. the day we honor soldiers who died for the United States is the fourth monday in may

30. president bill clinton took office in january of 1993

31. what holiday comes on the first monday in september

32. is there an abbreviation for may or july

Optional Exercise: Write a sentence in which you name your favorite month. Then write a sentence or two to tell why it is your favorite.

LESSON 16
Writing the Names of Holidays, Special Days, and Seasons

> **Handbook Guide 1i**
>
> **Begin the words that name holidays or special days with capital letters. Do not begin the name of a season with a capital letter.**

In the blank spaces opposite, write the following words as they should be written. Be very careful since some of them may be correct. Copy the correct words. Use a dictionary to find out about holidays you don't know. (Score: 18)

Examples:

| | christmas | *Christmas* _____ |
| | Summer | *summer* _____ |

1. presidents' day _____
2. independence day _____
3. tet _____
4. Winter _____
5. easter _____
6. mother's day _____
7. Halloween _____
8. new year's day _____
9. ramadan _____
10. Flag Day _____
11. Spring _____
12. kwanzaa _____
13. st. patrick's day _____
14. labor day _____
15. Autumn _____
16. thanksgiving day _____
17. Rosh Hashanah _____
18. memorial day _____

Optional Exercise: Write three sentences about what you like to do on holidays. Make sure to capitalize the name of each holiday.

LESSON 17
Capitalization

PART I   In the following sentences, draw a line under each uncapitalized word or abbreviation that should begin with a capital letter. (Score: 43)

Examples:

labor day is a holiday.   *some groups of people plant trees on arbor day.*

Holidays

1.   a favorite winter holiday in great britain is boxing day, the day after christmas.

2.   nick and i watched football on TV for nine hours on new year's day.

3.   the third monday in january is martin luther king day.

4.   the chinese new year often falls in february.

5.   do you wear green on st. patrick's day?

6.   why is april fools' day so popular with students?

7.   memorial day is celebrated throughout the united states.

8.   rosh hashanah, an important Jewish holiday, usually falls in september.

9.   isn't the ram's horn blown on rosh hashanah?

10.   little bairam is a Muslim festival celebrated at the end of a fast.

PART II   Write a sentence that tells something about each holiday or special day listed. You may use an encyclopedia to find needed information. (Score: 6)

11.   (Fourth of July)   _____

12.   (Cinco de Mayo)   _____

13.   (Valentine's Day)   _____

Connecting Meanings   _____

Draw a line from each word in row 1 to its meaning in row 2. Then write a sentence using each word in row 1.

Row 1   colander   calendar   cylinder

Row 2   shape that is long and round   food strainer   chart of days

LESSON 18
Using There Was *and* There Were

> **Handbook Guide 28c**
>
> Use *there was* or *was there* when speaking of one person or thing. Use *there were* or *were there* when speaking of more than one person or thing.

Fill each blank with *there was, there were, was there,* or *were there.*   (Score: 21)

The Legend of Helen of Troy

1. Once _____ a Greek king who married a woman named Helen.

2. _____ anyone more beautiful than she?

3. _____ a prince of Troy who carried Helen away.

4. Soon _____ many Greek soldiers outside the city of Troy.

5. For ten years _____ war between Greece and Troy.

6. _____ any famous heroes who fought in the battles?

7. _____ Achilles, who could be wounded only on his heel.

8. Also _____ Hector, the chief Trojan warrior.

9. What a fierce battle _____ between Hector and Achilles!

10. _____ many people killed besides Hector and Achilles?

11. _____ a clever plan developed by the Greeks?

12. _____ any soldiers left behind when the Greeks sailed their ships away?

13. _____ a giant wooden horse left outside the gates of Troy.

14. _____ a wild celebration after the horse was brought inside?

15. _____ some Trojans who feared that the gift was a trick?

16. _____ many who thought the horse was a tribute to the gods.

17. _____ Greek soldiers hiding inside the giant horse.

18. Late at night _____ no one to see them sneak out of hiding.

19. Inside the city walls _____ a last great battle.

20. _____ few Trojans left alive.

21. For Helen and King Menelaus _____ many peaceful years ahead.

UNIT II

LESSON 19
Writing Dates

Handbook Guides 5, 9

Place a comma between the day of the week and the month and between the day of the month and the year. Place a period after each abbreviation.

PART I Punctuate the following dates. (Score: 12)

Examples:

Jan. 5, 1914

Tuesday, May 12, 1998

Actress Courteney Cox was born on June 15, 1964.

1. January 2 1928
2. July 4 1900
3. April 19 1775
4. November 11 1918

5. Feb 14 1980
6. Nov 28 1969
7. Saturday April 4 1989
8. Monday January 2 1998

PART II Punctuate the dates in these sentences. (Score: 18)

As Time Goes By

9. Christopher Columbus set sail westward on August 3 1492.

10. He reached land on October 12 1492.

11. On July 16 1969, a spacecraft headed for the moon.

12. Neil Armstrong set foot on the moon on Sunday July 20 1969.

13. Valentina Tereshkova flew in a spacecraft from June 16 1963, to June 19 1963.

14. Miss Tereshkova was born on Saturday March 6 1937.

15. Another air pioneer, Amelia Earhart, was born on July 24 1898.

16. On May 20 1932, she began her famous solo flight across the Atlantic Ocean.

17. She disappeared on July 2 1937 while on a flight around the world.

18. Alexander Graham Bell sent the first voice message by wire on March 10 1876.

19. The first voice message was sent from space on December 18 1958.

20. The Pilgrims landed at Plymouth on December 21 1620.

21. Alaska became the forty-ninth state of the United States on January 3 1959.

22. On Friday August 21 1959, Hawaii became the fiftieth state.

UNIT II

LESSON 20
Choosing Standard Forms

Handbook Guide 28

Draw a line under the appropriate words in parentheses. (Score: 27)

The Monarch Mystery

1.   (There is, There are) an orange and black butterfly known as the monarch.

2.   These butterflies (is, are) a familiar sight in the eastern United States all summer.

3.   (Is, Are) these butterflies ever seen there in winter?

4.   The winter home of these butterflies (was, were) once a mystery.

5.   Norah and Fred Urquhart (is, are) two people who have studied the monarch.

6.   They (was, were) searching for the winter home of these butterflies.

7.   Fred Urquhart (was, were) working on the mystery sixty years ago.

8.   A butterfly (is, are) hard to tag.

9.   The Urquharts (was, were) able to tag thousands.

10. Fred and Norah (is, are) very careful people.

11. The butterflies (was, were) not harmed by the tags.

12. People (was, were) asked to look for tagged butterflies.

13. (There was, There were) many letters sent to the Urquharts.

14. It (was, were) learned that these butterflies won't fly at night.

15. Most monarchs (was, were) flying southwest in the fall.

16. People in Mexico (was, were) asked to help find the answer.

17. Ken Brugger (was, were) glad to help.

18. He and his dog (was, were) on the road looking for monarchs day after day.

19. By April of 1974 they (was, were) hot on the trail.

20. But the mystery (was, were) not solved then.

21. Ken (was, were) later joined by his wife, Kathy, who is from Mexico.

22. Tagged butterflies (was, were) found by Kathy and Ken in one area of Mexico.

23. The mystery (was, were) solved on January 9, 1975.

24. The monarchs (was, were) found in a mountain forest in central Mexico.

25. (There was, There were) millions of them resting on the trees.

26. Norah and Fred Urquhart (was, were) told quickly.

27. The Urquharts (was, were) very happy to learn of the monarchs' winter home.

Optional Exercise: Write sentences about butterflies. Use *is, are, was, were, there is, there are, there was,* and *there were.*

Name_____

LESSON 21
Writing Sentences Using the First-Person Voice

Handbook Guide 18a

A writer writes in the first-person voice, using the pronoun *I*, to tell about a personal experience.

A writer writes in the second-person voice, using the pronoun *you*, when speaking to someone else.

A writer writes in the third-person voice, using the pronouns *he*, *she*, and *it*, when writing as an outside observer.

Think About Sentences

There's more to learn about sentences. For example, did you know that a sentence can have a **voice**? Read these sentences and think about who the writer of each sentence must be. Then draw a line from each sentence to the person who must have written it.

1. I lost my wallet at the beach.   someone speaking directly to the person who lost the wallet

2. You lost your wallet at the beach.   an outside observer

3. He lost his wallet at the beach.   the person who lost the wallet

The first sentence is written in the **first person**. The writer is talking about something that happened to him, and he refers to himself as *I*.

The next sentence is written in the **second person**. The writer is talking directly to someone else, and he uses the word *you* to refer to that person.

The last sentence is written in the **third person**. This writer isn't really part of the picture. She is looking at the scene from the outside, which is why she uses the words *he* and *his*.

Read these sentences. Write **first person**, **second person**, or **third person** to show the voice of each sentence.

4. I went to the beach with Geraldo.   _____

5. Did Regina go with you, too?   _____

6. You should have worn sunscreen.   _____

7. He caught a crab in his net!   _____

8. Crab is my favorite food.   _____

9. Regina found Bill's wallet.   _____

10. I was relieved to hear that.   _____

Write Sentences

Now it's your turn to practice using a certain voice when you write. The questions below ask you to describe a place you like to spend time in. Write a complete sentence to answer each question, using the **first-person** voice. Use the word *I*, *me*, *my*, or *mine* in each sentence you write.

Example: What is your favorite sport?

My favorite sport is baseball.

11. What is your favorite place to relax? _____

    _____

12. Why do you like this place? _____

    _____

13. What are two things you usually do there? _____

    _____

14. Do you like to go there alone, or with others? _____

    _____

15. If you go with others, who are they? _____

    _____

16. How does this place make you feel? _____

    _____

Put Sentences Together

You can put all of the sentences you wrote together to make a **paragraph**. A paragraph is a group of sentences that all tell about the same idea, or topic. Read your sentences, one after the other. Do the ideas flow smoothly? Can you add or change any words that will make the sentences fit together better? Make some changes, if you like. Then, on another sheet of paper, write your sentences as a paragraph. Read over your paragraph. Would it give readers a feeling for why this place is special to you?

UNIT II

LESSON 22
Unit II Review

1. Write one asking sentence, one telling sentence, and one exclamatory sentence. (Score: 3)

   Handbook Guide 17

   _____

   _____

   _____

2. Write three questions, using in each the words given at the left. (Score: 3)

   Handbook Guide 28c

   was there   _____

   were there   _____

   is there   _____

3. Write the names of four days of the week and their abbreviations. (Score: 8)

   Handbook Guide 4

   _____   _____

   _____   _____

4. Write the names of four months and their abbreviations. (Score: 8)

   Handbook Guide 5

   _____   _____

   _____   _____

5. Write the names of four holidays. (Score: 4)

   Handbook Guide 1i

   _____   _____

   _____   _____

6. Rewrite these sentences, using capital letters and punctuation where needed. (Score: 9)

   Handbook Guides 1a, 1h, 1i, 9a, 17b, 17d

   is thanksgiving day always celebrated on a thursday   _____

   _____

   was the zoo opened on may 24 1996   _____

   _____

LESSON 23
Writing Abbreviations

> **Handbook Guides 3–5, 6b**
>
> **Capitalize abbreviations used in addresses. No period is needed after an abbreviation made of two or more capital letters.**

Write the abbreviation for each of the following words that can be abbreviated. Put an X on the line when the word cannot be abbreviated. (Score: 36)

Examples:

Mister *Mr.*_____   June   *X*_____

1. Street _____   19. December _____
2. February _____   20. Tuesday _____
3. Thursday _____   21. September _____
4. August _____   22. Saturday _____
5. East _____   23. Reverend _____
6. October _____   24. North _____
7. Doctor _____   25. Judge _____
8. November _____   26. Wednesday _____
9. Monday _____   27. May _____
10. April _____   28. Southeast _____
11. Friday _____   29. Colonel _____
12. Northeast _____ 30. July _____
13. Sunday _____   31. President _____
14. West _____   32. Northwest _____
15. March _____   33. Avenue _____
16. Miss _____   34. January _____
17. Southwest _____ 35. Governor _____
18. Professor _____ 36. Boulevard _____

Optional Exercise: Write five sentences, using five of the words above.

Name_____   Perfect Score 34   My Score _____

LESSON 24
Writing Contractions

Handbook Guide 13

When you combine two words to form a contraction, use an apostrophe (') to show where letters are left out.

Read the two sentences below.

     A foot-long chili dog *is not* a light snack.
     A foot-long chili dog *isn't* a light snack.

Is there any difference between the sentences? In the second sentence, the words *is* and *not* have been combined to form a contraction. What letter has been left out?

In the blank spaces, write the contractions for the following words. (Score: 34)

1.	are not	_____	18. should not	_____
2.	was not	_____	19. they are	_____
3.	you will	_____	20. she will	_____
4.	do not	_____	21. has not	_____
5.	we have	_____	22. you have	_____
6.	would not	_____	23. he is	_____
7.	we are	_____	24. have not	_____
8.	that is	_____	25. I have	_____
9.	did not	_____	26. he will	_____
10.	she is	_____	27. you are	_____
11.	had not	_____	28. is not	_____
12.	they will	_____	29. I am	_____
13.	were not	_____	30. will not	_____
14.	they have	_____	31. I will	_____
15.	could not	_____	32. cannot	_____
16.	we will	_____	33. it is	_____
17.	who is	_____	34. does not	_____

LESSON 25
Using Contractions

> **Handbook Guides 13, 28**
>
> Use *isn't* or *wasn't* when you speak of one person or thing. Use *aren't* or *weren't* when you speak of more than one person or thing.

Draw a line under the appropriate word in parentheses in each sentence. (Score: 19)

Diamond Cutters

1.   Rough diamonds (isn't, aren't) beautiful jewels.

2.   (Isn't, Aren't) it hard to cut and polish diamonds?

3.   (Isn't, Aren't) people surprised to see a diamond the size of a walnut?

4.   (Isn't, Aren't) that diamond worth thousands of dollars?

5.   Why (isn't, aren't) that diamond ready to be polished?

6.   It (isn't, aren't) a perfect diamond.

7.   A diamond with a flaw in it (isn't, aren't) clear and bright.

8.   Flaws (isn't, aren't) easy to see without a magnifying glass.

9.   It (isn't, aren't) easy to cut a large diamond in half.

10. Shattered diamonds (isn't, aren't) worth much.

11. The diamond cutter (isn't, aren't) ready to cut this diamond.

12. (Isn't, Aren't) it important to study a diamond before cutting it?

13. The diamond cutter (isn't, aren't) sure where to hit this diamond.

14. (Isn't, Aren't) the diamond cutter holding a mallet and a wedge?

15. (Isn't, Aren't) this person afraid of making a one-hundred-thousand-dollar mistake?

16. The diamond cutter's hands (isn't, aren't) shaking.

17. The diamond cutter (isn't, aren't) at all nervous.

18. The tapping noises (isn't, aren't) loud.

19. (Isn't, Aren't) it amazing to see a diamond cut in half perfectly?

Odd Word Out _____

Circle the word in this list that does not belong with the others. Name a category that would fit the four uncircled words. Then name a category for the word you circled.

amethyst   ocelot   garnet   opal   sapphire

UNIT III

LESSON 26
Using Their, There, *and* They're

Handbook Guides 13, 33

Their shows possession or ownership. *There* means "in that place." *There* is often used to begin a sentence. *They're* is a contraction of *they are*.

Fill in the blank spaces with *their*, *there*, or *they're*. (Score: 19)

Example:

Look at the model over ____*there*____ .

The boys are completing ____*their*____ project.

____*They're*____ putting on the finishing touches now.

The Tinker's Workshop

1.   In Berkeley, California, _____ is a special place for budding inventors.

2.   The Tinker's Workshop is a place for people of all ages to test _____ ideas.

3.   _____ is no charge for a visit to the Tinker's Workshop.

4.   Visitors are asked to bring only _____ imagination.

5.   Look at those two girls over _____.

6.   _____ building a nine-foot robot.

7.   A toy from Japan provided inspiration for _____ idea.

8.   Nick Bertoni, the workshop's founder, helps visitors with _____ plans.

9.   Mr. Bertoni keeps drills, torches, and other tools _____ on the counter.

10.   _____ placed _____ for anyone to use.

11.   _____ is just one requirement at the Tinker's Workshop.

12.   Every item built _____ must be an original invention.

13.   The two boys over _____ are building a mechanical firefly.

14.   _____ part of the Young Inventors Program, which meets on Saturdays.

15.   They plan to enter _____ unusual invention in a science fair about robots.

16.   Inventors share _____ ideas in a series of talks at the Tinker's Workshop.

17.   _____ is a small fee for attending the talks.

18.   People who have come to the talks agree that _____ well worth the money.

LESSON 27
Using May *and* Can

Handbook Guide 30
Use *may* to give permission. Use *can* to show that you are able to do something.

Fill each blank space with *may* or *can*. (Score: 19)

Examples:

_____ *May* _____ I have a pickle?

I _____ *can* _____ always eat a pickle.

1. Yes, you _____ help yourself to one of my pickles.

2. _____ you imagine how they taste?

3. _____ I offer you my recipe for vinegar pickles?

4. I _____ help you learn how to make delicious pickles.

5. _____ you wait seven months to eat the pickles?

6. _____ I give you some cucumbers that have been soaking in salt water?

7. _____ you rinse them in fresh water for me?

8. _____ I show you which spices I use?

9. No one _____ make good pickles without spices.

10. I _____ make many different kinds of pickles.

11. Pickles _____ be stored for a long time.

12. You _____ pickle many vegetables besides cucumbers.

13. _____ I give you some pickled cabbage to try?

14. I _____ also let you try some pickled radishes.

15. _____ I open a jar of pickled chili peppers for you?

16. I _____ hardly wait for you to try one.

17. _____ you tell me which store sells crunchy pickles?

18. _____ I offer you something that is unusual?

19. You _____ have another scoop of pickle ice cream, if you wish.

LESSON 28
Using A and An

> **Handbook Guide 29**
>
> Use *an* before a word that begins with a vowel sound. Use *a* before a word that begins with a consonant sound.

In the sentences below, fill each blank with *a* or *an*. (Score: 17)

Examples:

This is _____*an*_____ ocean beach.

Sheila studied marine biology at _____*a*_____ university.

Shark!

1. *Jaws* was certainly _____ exciting movie.

2. Wasn't that movie about _____ white shark?

3. The white shark is _____ unusually large and dangerous fish.

4. _____ ocean beach can be _____ dangerous place to swim.

5. One of these sea beasts may see _____ arm or _____ leg moving.

6. Blood from _____ open wound may draw these fish near.

7. These hunters of the deep will swallow _____ number of things.

8. One blue shark was found to have swallowed _____ old kettle.

9. That fish also swallowed _____ jar of nails.

10. It had even swallowed _____ roll of tar paper!

11. _____ shark is _____ creature that never gets cancer.

12. Many scientists are taking _____ interest in this fact.

13. These fish don't seem to show _____ old-age stage of life, either.

14. Perhaps chemicals from sharks will have _____ use in medicine someday.

Word Whiz _____

Use the clues on the left to help you complete the words on the right. Use a dictionary for spelling help.

animal that eats other animals   p r __ __ __ t o r

animal that is eaten by other animals   p r __ __

Writing: Use the words you wrote in two sentences about sharks.

LESSON 29
Writing Titles

Copy the following titles, using capital letters where they should be used. (Score: 36—2 for each title)

Example:

sports in america _____*Sports in America*_____

1. you are the sunshine of my life _____

2. the legend of sleepy hollow _____

3. the call of the wild _____

4. solomon's seal _____

5. fiddler on the roof _____

6. the red pony _____

7. a brief history of time _____

8. war of the worlds _____

9. the three musketeers _____

10. lincoln at gettysburg _____

11. number the stars _____

12. i will always love you _____

13. jurassic park _____

14. a day no pigs would die _____

15. the pied piper of hamelin _____

16. this land is your land _____

17. the last emperor _____

18. stranger in a strange land _____

Optional Exercise: Write the title of your favorite song.

Name_____   Perfect Score 36   My Score _____

LESSON 30
Punctuation and Capitalization

Rewrite these sentences in the blank spaces. Be careful to use capital letters and punctuation marks where they are needed. (Score: 36)

Example:

annie oakley was from darke county ohio   *Annie Oakley was from Darke County, Ohio*

Annie Oakley

1. annie's real name was phoebe anne oakley mozee   _____

    _____

2. her birth date is august 13 1860   _____

    _____

3. did annie win a shooting contest when she was fifteen   _____

    _____

4. was it held in cincinnati ohio   _____

    _____

5. annie oakley later went on tour with buffalo bill   _____

    _____

6. she starred in the united states and in other countries   _____

    _____

7. annie could slice a playing card in two with one shot   _____

    _____

8. she would also shoot at the heart on the ace of hearts   _____

    _____

9. could she put five shots through it as it fell   _____

    _____

10. how quickly annie fired those shots   _____

    _____

LESSON 31
Choosing Standard Forms

Draw a line under the appropriate word in parentheses. (Score: 30)

The Exercise Program

1. I have (began, begun) to watch an aerobics show on TV.
2. This show (learns, teaches) people how to become agile and fit.
3. I (have, has) been a couch potato lately.
4. The host of the show (doesn't, don't) look like a couch potato.
5. I want the host to (learn, teach) me all the secrets of aerobic training.
6. The viewers (does, do) the exercises along with the host.
7. Not all of the exercises (is, are) easy.
8. This morning we (learned, taught) a new exercise.
9. The new exercise (is, are) the six-count stoop.
10. I (wrote, written) notes on how to do this exercise.
11. Then I (began, begun) to do the exercise.
12. Six-count stoops (is, are) very tiring.
13. The host (sang, sung) a song while exercising.
14. I couldn't even have (sang, sung) "Mary Had a Little Lamb."
15. My breath was completely (gone, went).
16. I (gone, went) to the refrigerator for a snack.
17. I (were, was) startled when the host yelled, "Come back here!"
18. I (took, taken) my hand off the ice cream.
19. I (run, ran) back to the TV set.
20. The host of the show (began, begun) to roll.
21. The picture on the screen also (began, begun) to roll.
22. Then my eyes (began, begun) to roll, and I felt dizzy.
23. I (gave, given) a sigh and (fell, fallen) to the floor.
24. It has (took, taken) me all day to recover.
25. At first I thought my arm was (broke, broken).
26. I hope I (do, does) better tomorrow morning.
27. Perhaps I can (become, became) as fit as the host.
28. Then I will (teach, learn) others the secrets of aerobics.
29. My pupils (isn't, aren't) going to snack on ice cream, either.

Name_____

LESSON 32
Writing Sentences That Compare

Think About Sentences

Handbook Guides 18a, 39

To show how things are different, use words such as *but, unlike, more, less, bigger, smaller, better, worse, earlier,* and *later.*

To show how things are alike or similar, use words such as *like* and *both.*

Sentences can be used in many ways. For example, you can use sentences to compare how two things are alike, or how they are different. The sentences below compare dogs and cats. Write **different** next to the sentences that describe how dogs and cats are different. Write **alike** next to the sentences that tell how these two animals are alike.

1. Dogs are members of the canine family, but cats are felines. _____

2. Scientists think that both cats and dogs are descendants of an ancient weasel-like creature called *Miacis.* _____

3. Dogs were tamed about 4,500 years earlier than cats. _____

4. Dogs were used mostly for hunting, but cats were used to control rat and snake populations. _____

5. Both dogs and cats must be trained. _____

6. Unlike dogs, most cats learn to follow only a very limited number of commands. _____

Words such as *but, unlike, more,* and *less* are often used in sentences that describe differences. Comparing words such as *bigger, better, worse,* and *earlier* are often used when describing differences.

Words such as *like* and *both* are often used in sentences that describe similarities.

Look back at the sentences above. Circle the word in each sentence that lets you know whether a difference or a similarity is being described.

Write Sentences

Now write your own sentences that compare dogs and cats. The words by the numbers tell you whether to describe a similarity or a difference. Use the comparing word in parentheses in the sentence you write.

Example:
difference
(use *better* or *worse*)   *Cats are better hunters than dogs.*

7. difference
   (use *but*)

   _____

8. difference
   (use *unlike*)

   _____

9. difference
   (use *more* or *less*)

   _____

   _____

Example:
similarity
(use *both*)   *Both dogs and cats have been helpful to humans over time.*

10. similarity
    (use *both*)

    _____

11. similarity
    (use *like*)

    _____

12. similarity
    (use *both*)

    _____

    _____

Put Sentences Together

You can combine the sentences in this lesson into two **paragraphs** that compare dogs and cats. It's easy. First, group all the sentences that describe how dogs and cats are alike. Those sentences will make up the first paragraph. Next, group all the sentences that tell how dogs and cats are different. These sentences will make up the second paragraph.

On another piece of paper, write the paragraphs. Use some of the sentences you wrote, and some of the sentences on page 38. Choose which sentences you want to include. Put the sentences in an order that makes sense. If you like, change some words so the sentences fit together better. You'll also need to add a sentence to the beginning of each paragraph that tells readers what the paragraph is about. Try these sentences:

For the first paragraph: In many ways, dogs and cats are alike.

For the second paragraph: Dogs and cats also are different in many ways.

Name_____   Perfect Score 40   My Score _____

LESSON 33
Unit III Review

1.   Write the abbreviations for the following words: **Handbook Guides 3–5, 6b**
     Saturday, December, Street, Avenue, North, Doctor,
     Southwest. (Score: 7)

     _____

2.   Write the contractions for these words. (Score: 12)   **Handbook Guide 13**

     they are _____   will not _____   I will   _____

     has not _____   does not _____   it is   _____

     is not _____   are not _____   were not _____

     was not _____   that is _____   we have _____

3.   Write five sentences, using a word at the left in each   **Handbook Guides 30, 33**
     sentence. (Score: 5)

     there   _____

     they're   _____

     their   _____

     may   _____

     can   _____

4.   Write three words that can be used after *a* and three   **Handbook Guide 29**
     that can be used after *an*. (Score: 6)

     a _____   a _____   a _____

     an _____   an _____   an _____

5.   On the lines below, write the titles of two songs, two   **Handbook Guide 7**
     movies, or two books that you remember. Use capital
     letters where they should be used. (Score: 2)

     _____   _____

6.   Rewrite this sentence, using capital letters and   **Handbook Guides 1b, 6c, 9a**
     commas where needed. (Score: 8)

     maria tallchief was born on january 24 1925 in fairfax oklahoma. _____

     _____

LESSON 34
Using Commas

In the following sentences, place commas where they are needed. (Score: 28)

Example:

Guam is an island Kate.

Guam is an island, Kate.

Guam

1. Amy did Magellan discover Guam?

2. You should read up on the subject Don.

3. Do you like to swim Amy?

4. I do, but I might step on a stonefish Don.

5. You'll be safe Amy if you wear these rubber-soled shoes.

6. Don let's forget swimming and go to the Spanish fort.

7. We'll go through the three cities of Agana Agat and Asan on the way.

8. Amy let's get something to eat before we leave.

9. I know a clean quiet restaurant.

10. I can try the *lumpia* Amy and you can try the chicken.

11. *Lumpia* is made of chopped vegetables chicken and shrimp.

12. *Kelaguin* red rice and *tuba* are three items that will surely be on the menu.

13. Don isn't *tuba* the sap of a coconut palm?

14. It has a warm salty lemony taste.

15. There are many other good foods on this island Amy.

16. Don let's see the fort and eat later.

17. I haven't eaten for three hours Amy.

18. I might want Filipino Mexican or Chinese food.

19. I've heard that Filipino food is somewhat like Mexican food Amy.

20. Since you are so hungry Don why don't you get all three?

Optional Exercise: Read about another country that is an island and tell your family something you learn about it. Use an encyclopedia for information.

Name_____ Perfect Score 28 My Score _____

LESSON 35
Using Troublesome Words

Handbook Guides 16, 28, 30, 33

Draw a line under the appropriate word in parentheses. (Score: 28)

Stunting for Money

1. Would you like (to, too, two) be a stunt person?
2. Maybe you have (red, read) that most stars don't try dangerous falls or car chases.
3. John Sharrod (is, are) a stunt man.
4. He (gave, given) up his job as a teacher to work in Hollywood.
5. Sharrod (has, have) been in several movies about Africa.
6. He has (took, taken) some awful falls.
7. He has stormed through burning buildings, (to, too, two).
8. Stunt people must plan (their, there) work carefully.
9. They (don't, doesn't) want to get hurt.
10. (There, Their) are many things that can go wrong during a dangerous stunt.
11. (It's, Its) not unusual for a stunt person to break a bone.
12. Stunt man Hal Needham (has, have) broken more than forty.
13. In one movie Needham (gone, went) on quite a ride.
14. He had (to, too, two) jump his pickup truck across a lake.
15. Needham made his truck more powerful (by, buy) putting in a rocket engine.
16. The rocket engine could have (blew, blown) the rear end off the pickup.
17. But (there, their) were no real problems with the stunt.
18. Kitty O'Neil (doesn't, don't) mind jumping out of airplanes.
19. She must be careful not to be (blew, blown) (to, too, two) far by the wind.
20. O'Neil has (took, taken) the wheel of a 300-mph supercar.
21. She (may, can) do trick diving off the high board, too.
22. Stunt people (is, are) proud of (there, their) skills.
23. But (there, their) are easier ways to make a living.
24. Would you like to be (threw, thrown) from a horse (to, too, two) dozen times?
25. People who (is, are) good at stunting can make good money.

Name That Job _____

Decide what occupation the person who uses these things probably has. Then write a paragraph describing how these items are used.

      set   clapstick   screenplay   cast

LESSON 36
Learning about Friendly Letters

PART I See if you can name the parts of this letter. Write the name of each part on the numbered line leading to it. (Score: 10—2 for each name)

107 Crescent Street

1. _____ Waltham, MA 02154

   June 18, 1998

2. _____ Dear Mel,

   Remember that book about stained-glass windows

3. _____ you sent me? Well, I did more than read it. I used it.

   As a matter of fact, I just finished making my first

   stained-glass window! What a great gift that book was!

4. _____ Your friend,

5. _____ Leslie

PART II Punctuate the following letter. Draw a line under each word that should begin with a capital letter and under any abbreviations that should be capitalized. (Score: 20)

6610 river street

eugene or 97401

december 11 1998

dear wendy

   everyone back here in eugene misses you very much. we hope you and your family are happy in wichita. is there any chance that you'll be able to come back here for a visit next summer? you would be most welcome to stay at our house

sincerely yours,

rebecca

Name_____   Perfect Score 25   My Score _____

LESSON 37
Writing a Friendly Letter

Rewrite this letter in the space below. Write the five parts of the letter in their proper places. Use commas and capital letters where they are needed. (Score: 25—5 points for each part correctly placed, punctuated, and capitalized)

                                        dear angela

778 park avenue
cleveland oh 44106
august 3 1998
stan
your friend
        would you like to sing in our Veterans day program? our choral group, the Singing Steelworkers, will sing seven songs. we would like you to sing two or three songs as a soloist. let me know soon if you'd like to participate.

_____

_____

_____

_____

_____

_____

_____

_____

_____

_____

Optional Exercise: Read Handbook Guide 23. Then write a business letter to a veterans' organization in your community. Ask for information on Veterans' Day celebrations in your area.

LESSON 38
Writing Envelope Addresses

PART I In the space below, address an envelope from Sally Blatchford, who lives at 802 Dale Avenue, Cincinnati, Ohio 45203, to Miss Kim Okamura, who lives at 4136 Quincy Street, Mercer Island, Washington 98040. Remember to use postal code abbreviations for the names of states when addressing envelopes. (Score: 10—5 points for each part correctly written)

PART II In the space below, address an envelope from Ms. Geri Gonzales, who lives at 77 Glen Avenue, Oakland, California 94611, to Mr. James Parsons, who lives at 243 Hill Street, New Albany, Indiana 47150. (Score: 10—5 points for each part correctly written)

Name_____   Perfect Score 21   My Score _____

LESSON 39
Using Saw *and* Seen

Write *saw* or *seen* in each blank. (Score: 21)

Pictures from Space

1.   Have you _____ the photographs taken during the Mars Pathfinder mission?

2.   I _____ some of those pictures on TV.

3.   Before Pathfinder's journey, the world had _____ only distant images of the red planet.

4.   Now many people have _____ the surface of Mars in great detail.

5.   They have _____ the dusty, reddish landscape that looks somewhat like deserts here on Earth.

6.   I _____ craters, rocks, and mountains.

7.   In one photograph I _____ a rock the scientists had named Casper.

8.   I also have _____ the rock they named Scooby Doo.

9.   People all over the world _____ little Sojourner snapping pictures.

10.   Most viewers _____ only a bleak landscape.

11.   Scientists, however, have _____ signs that once Mars may have supported life.

12.   Scientists believe that Mars _____ warmer, wetter days in its ancient past.

13.   The passing centuries have _____ great changes happen on this lonely planet.

14.   The planet we have _____ through Sojourner's photographs is bitterly cold.

15.   I have never _____ a bleaker-looking place.

16.   Have you _____ the images of Europa, Jupiter's smallest moon?

17.   I _____ some pictures taken by the space probe Galileo.

18.   Scientists _____ strange slushy formations on Europa's frozen surface.

19.   Some who have _____ these believe there may be a liquid ocean beneath the frozen crust.

20.   We have _____ some beautiful pictures from outer space in recent years.

21.   The pictures I _____ yesterday are the most amazing ones yet.

LESSON 40
Using Did *and* Done

Handbook Guide 16

Did is never used with a helping word. *Done* is used with a helping word such as *has, have, had, is, are, was,* or *were.*

Write *did* or *done* in each blank. (Score: 18)

1. _____ you see the February 1988 issue of *National Geographic* magazine?

2. What have you _____ with it?

3. What _____ you think of Mary Ellen Mark's photography?

4. Has anyone ever _____ such strong portraits of the people of Sydney, Australia?

5. How _____ Mary Ellen Mark begin her work?

6. _____ she grow up in Philadelphia?

7. In college she _____ some artwork.

8. But she _____ not think she would ever be a great painter.

9. She _____ feel that she had a chance to be a good photographer, however.

10. By 1969 she had _____ enough work to win a job with the magazine *Look.*

11. Ms. Mark has also _____ work for *Esquire, Time, Ms.,* and *Newsweek.*

12. Most of her work is _____ with a 35mm camera.

13. She _____ a powerful photo essay on Northern Ireland.

14. Perhaps you have _____ some photography.

15. What _____ you choose to photograph?

16. _____ you have any trouble focusing the camera?

17. I just _____ something I've always wanted to do.

18. I've _____ a photo essay on pizza chefs.

Word Whiz Use the clues on the left to help you complete the words on the right. Use a dictionary for spelling help.

lens that enlarges   __ __ __ __ p h o t o

looks good in pictures   p h o t o __ __ __ __ __

plant process   p h o t o __ __ __ __ __ s i s

UNIT IV

LESSON 41
Punctuation and Capitalization

Punctuate the sentences below. Draw a line under each uncapitalized word that should begin with a capital letter. You do not need to add quotation marks. (Score: 84)

Example:

<u>minnesota</u> is almost in the middle of <u>north</u> <u>america</u>.

The Land of Ten Thousand Lakes

1.   tell us something amazing about minnesota phil

2.   almost everything about minnesota is amazing

3.   its name comes from the language of the Dakota Nation

4.   does that word mean "sky-blue water"?

5.   phil does minnesota really have ten thousand lakes

6.   it actually has more than fifteen thousand lakes

7.   the sport of water-skiing was developed in minnesota

8.   what an exciting sport it is

9.   isn't the source of the mississippi river in minnesota

10. is the mississippi the longest river in north america

11. how I wish I could take a canoe trip this week

12. duluth minneapolis and mankato are cities in minnesota

13. phil aren't you from hibbing

14. hibbing is a rather famous small town in minnesota

15. hibbing was the childhood home of bob dylan

16. didn't he write a song called "forever young"

17. how cold is the weather in hibbing in january

18. it's sometimes forty degrees below zero Fahrenheit

19. I really miss the cold crisp fresh air

20. do people stay indoors when it's that cold phil

21. a few people take long fast rides on snowmobiles

22. can you name two minnesotans who became vice presidents of the united states

23. hubert horatio humphrey and walter mondale are their names

LESSON 42
Choosing Standard Forms

Draw a line under the appropriate word or words in parentheses. (Score: 27)

Recording Stars

1. (Who's, Whose) the violin player in the Dave Matthews Band?

2. (Isn't, Aren't) his name Boyd Tinsley?

3. The others in the group (is, are) drummer Carter Beauford, saxophonist Leroi Moore, bassist Stefan Lessard, and Matthews, who plays guitar.

4. (Isn't, Aren't) Dave Matthews originally from South Africa?

5. Haven't you (saw, seen) the band perform?

6. I (saw, seen) them in Charlotte, North Carolina, last year.

7. (There is, There are) few groups as exciting on stage as this band is.

8. (There, Their, They're) popular with fans all around the country.

9. (There, Their, They're) music has a Celtic flavor and strong, complex rhythms.

10. (May, Can) you dance to it?

11. (May, Can) I borrow your *Crash* CD?

12. (Is, Are) the band members going to record a new CD soon?

13. I have never (saw, seen) a recording session.

14. (Its, It's) not easy to make a good recording.

15. The long sessions (is, are) hard on the singers' voices.

16. (Who's, Whose) microphone is buzzing?

17. It has taken almost (to, too, two) weeks to record that song.

18. (Was there, Were there) a reason for choosing that song to record?

19. None of the singers likes (its, it's) melody.

20. But (there, their, they're) all hoping it will be a hit.

21. The musicians have (a, an) idea.

22. That song needs (a, an) powerful beat (to, too, two) put it over.

23. The musicians will add an electric bass and maybe congas, (to, too, two).

24. (Is, Are) the singers really wearing earplugs?

25. Did they say that the high notes hurt (there, their, they're) ears?

26. By tomorrow the vocal tracks will have been (did, done).

LESSON 43
Using the Writing Process to Write a Science Report

Handbook Guide 20
The steps in writing a science report are:
Choose a topic
Gather information
Make an outline
Write and revise
Proofread
Publish

Read a Science Report

In this lesson you will learn how to write a science report that is one paragraph long. A science report gives facts about a topic in nature. Here are some guidelines for writing a paragraph of science facts.

- Begin your paragraph with a sentence that tells what the **topic** is. This is called the **topic sentence.**

- Present **facts** about your topic in the main part, or **body**, of the paragraph.

- Use **formal language**, the kind of language you might find in a textbook. Do not use informal expressions or slang.

- Use **scientific terms** that have to do with the topic. Make sure you spell these words correctly.

- End your paragraph with a **concluding sentence** that sums up your main point.

- **The steps of the Writing Process** in this lesson will help you plan, write, revise, and correct your report.

Read this example of a short science report:

The Sea's Most Fearsome Predator

   This report will explain why sharks are such successful hunters. First, sharks have an amazing ability to find prey. They have a fluid-filled canal called a lateral line. It runs down both sides of their bodies from head to tail. Scientists think that sharks use this canal to feel water movement and low-pitched sounds. This ability helps a shark find prey even when it can't see it. Also, sharks can sense electrical fields through tiny pores on their heads. This ability lets sharks feel the presence of fish, because fish give out small bits of electricity when they move. Sharks can also find prey just by looking for it. They can see very well, even in the dim underwater light of the sea. Once the prey has been found, sharks are masters at chasing, biting, and devouring. A shark's sleek body is shaped like a torpedo. This helps the shark speed through the water. Its strong, curved tail and fins help it move very fast while chasing prey. Speed, strength, and bite power make the shark a fearsome predator.

Complete these items about the report above.

1. What is the topic of the report? _____

2. Underline the topic sentence. (This sentence tells readers what the report will explain.)

3. Draw a box around at least one scientific word.

4. Draw a star next to the concluding sentence.

5. Put an X by the first word of the paragraph. It appears several spaces in from the left margin. The first sentence of a paragraph should always be **indented** like this.

Write a Science Report

Now you'll have a chance to write your own short science report. Follow the steps of the **Writing Process** given below.

I.   Choose a Topic

Choose a topic that is not too big. "Sea Creatures" is too big a topic to cover in a paragraph. "How Dolphins Communicate" or "How Tides Work" would be a better topic. Write down three or four topic ideas. Circle the idea you like best.

_____   _____

_____   _____

II.   Gather Information

Find two or more books from which to gather information. You can use library books, the encyclopedia, or textbooks. You can also find information on the Internet. Once you've found the information you're looking for, skim it to look for answers to questions such as these: *Where* is the plant or animal found? *What* is unique about it?

III.   Make an Outline

Decide what information you want to give about your topic. You will only have room for some of the facts. Organize your facts in an outline or list.

IV.   Write and Revise

Use your outline to write a first draft of your report. Do this on another piece of paper. Don't worry about mistakes. You'll have a chance to fix them later.

Read over your first draft. Ask yourself these questions:

- Does the paragraph begin with a topic sentence that tells what the report is about?
- Do all the details in the body of the paragraph give more information about the topic?
- Does the paragraph have a concluding sentence that sums up the main point?
- Should I add or take out anything?
- Is the report interesting and fun to read?

Now make changes that will strengthen your report.

V.   Proofread

Do a final check of your work. Make sure you have spelled every word correctly, especially scientific words. Also make sure you have used capital letters correctly. Remember that the first sentence of your paragraph should be indented.

VI.   Publish

After you've corrected your report, make a clean copy. Write it over by hand, or use a word processor. Share your writing with your teacher, or parent, or a friend.

Name_____   Perfect Score 40   My Score _____

LESSON 44
Unit IV Review

1. After each word below, write a word having the same sound but a different meaning. (Score: 4)   **Handbook Guide 33**

    its _____   buy _____   two _____   whose _____

2. Name the parts of a friendly letter. (Score: 5)   **Handbook Guide 22a**

    a. _____   b. _____   c. _____

    d. _____   e. _____

3. Rewrite the letter heading below, using capital letters and commas where needed. (Score: 7)   **Handbook Guide 22b**

    424 maple avenue   _____

    kokomo in 46901   _____

    june 21 2000   _____

4. Write two sentences, using the pair of words given at the left in each sentence. (Score: 4)   **Handbook Guide 16**

    saw, did   _____

    seen, done   _____

5. Rewrite these sentences, using capital letters and punctuation where needed. (Score: 10)   **Handbook Guides 1a, 1b, 10, 12, 17b–e**

    how dark that cloud is   _____

    we have planted radishes onions and lettuce   _____

    _____

    did you weed the garden this morning jane   _____

    _____

6. Write two sentences. In one, include the name of the person you are writing to. In the other, name three different things you often buy at a grocery store. (Score: 10)   **Handbook Guides 1a, 1b, 10, 12**

    _____

    _____

    _____

LESSON 45
Punctuating Direct Quotations

In the following sentences, place commas where they are needed. (Score: 19)

Handbook Guide 8

Use a comma to separate a quotation from the words that tell who said it, unless the quotation is a question or an exclamation that comes before the words that tell who said it.

Example:

Nick said, "I'll tell you about a haunted house."

"You'll shiver with fright!" he then exclaimed. *(No comma is needed.)*

1. Shelley asked "Is this a true story?"

2. Nick replied "Yes, it's true."

3. "There was a large, desolate house in Aachen" said Nick.

4. "That's a town in Germany" said Shelley.

5. "No one had lived in the house for five years" Nick said.

6. Jan asked "Why didn't anyone live there?"

7. Nick answered "Mysterious sounds came from the house."

8. "No one could explain the loud noises" he added.

9. "Was someone secretly living there?" asked Shelley.

10. "No, the house was carefully searched several times" replied Nick.

11. "I wouldn't have been afraid" said Shelley.

12. "But most people were afraid" Nick said to Shelley.

13. "Why didn't some brave person buy the house?" she asked.

14. Nick replied "The house was finally sold for a low price."

15. "Did the noises torment the new owner?" asked Jan.

16. Nick said "The new owner found the cause of the sounds."

17. "A window in one room was broken" Nick said.

18. "The door to that room had a broken latch" he continued.

19. Shelley said "I know! When the wind blew hard, the door would bang."

20. Nick said "Once the door and window were fixed, the noises stopped."

21. Jan said "I can tell you why the noises stopped."

22. "The ghosts must have felt unwelcome after the repairs were made" Jan explained.

23. "What a hopeless case you are!" groaned Shelley.

Name_____ Perfect Score 44 My Score _____

LESSON 46
Using Quotation Marks

In the following sentences, place quotation marks where they are needed. (Score: 44)

Example:

"Who was the greatest heavyweight boxer in history?" asked Ralph.

Heavyweight Champions of the World

1. Muhammad Ali was certainly the greatest, said Toni.

2. He thought he was, but I'm not sure, said Ralph.

3. Well, he knocked out Sonny Liston twice, said Lee.

4. Toni said, Joe Frazier and George Foreman were great boxers.

5. But Ali knocked out both of them, she added.

6. What about the great champions of earlier eras? asked Ralph.

7. Lee said, Rocky Marciano did retire undefeated in 1956.

8. Toni asked, Didn't Marciano beat some pretty good boxers?

9. Ralph said He beat Ezzard Charles, Archie Moore, and Jersey Joe Walcott.

10. Lee said, Joe Louis was a great champion for many years.

11. He won twenty-six title bouts in a row, Ralph said.

12. Have either of you heard of Jack Dempsey? asked Lee.

13. He beat that giant, Jess Willard, didn't he? asked Toni.

14. Ralph said, Dad's grandmother was a real boxing fan.

15. She saw Dempsey knock out Luis Firpo in 1923, he continued.

16. Lee said, That fight didn't even go two rounds.

17. Let's not leave out Jack Johnson, said Toni.

18. He held the heavyweight title for seven years, Ralph said.

19. But I still think Muhammad Ali was the greatest, said Toni.

20. She continued, He floated like a butterfly and stung like a bee.

21. Ralph said, Joe Louis would have swatted Ali with one punch.

22. Not a chance! exclaimed Toni.

LESSON 47
Writing Singular and
Plural Forms of Words

PART I   Write the plural forms of the following words. (Score: 20)

Examples:

hat *hats*   watch *watches*   man *men*   spy *spies*

1.   wheel   _____
2.   dog   _____
3.   book   _____
4.   pencil   _____
5.   brush   _____
6.   lunch   _____
7.   leaf   _____
8.   loaf   _____
9.   calf   _____
10.   knife   _____

11.   life   _____
12.   lily   _____
13.   baby   _____
14.   berry   _____
15.   toy   _____
16.   donkey   _____
17.   child   _____
18.   ox   _____
19.   tooth   _____
20.   sheep   _____

PART II   In each blank write the plural form of the word in parentheses. (Score: 10)

Example:

(place) An earthquake shook some places in California in 1994.

21.   (valley) The quake was felt in Los Angeles and in the _____ nearby.

22.   (cry) Many _____ of fear were heard during the quake.

23.   (woman) Fifty-seven people were killed, and a number of children, _____, and men were injured.

24.   (bridge) Were any _____ damaged by the shock waves?

25.   (freeway) Sections of some of the _____ collapsed due to the quake.

26.   (shelf) Books were knocked from _____ by the quake.

27.   (dish) In some houses, many _____ were broken.

28.   (way) Someday we may have better _____ to predict earthquakes.

29.   (mouse) Do _____ act strange just before an earthquake?

30.   (fish) Can _____ sense that a quake is about to happen?

Name_____   Perfect Score 24   My Score _____

LESSON 48
Writing Singular and Plural Words

PART I In each of the following sentences, a word has been underlined. Some of the words are singular, and some are plural. If an underlined word is singular, write its plural form in the blank. If the word is plural, write its singular form. (Score: 10)

Examples:

A group of cattle is a <u>herd</u>.   *herds*

A bunch of <u>monkeys</u> is called a troop.   *monkey*

1. Have you ever heard of a gaggle of <u>geese</u>?   _____

2. You can also call a group of geese a <u>flock</u>.   _____

3. *Flock* is also the word for a bunch of <u>sheep</u>. _____

4. What is a <u>bunch</u> of lions called?   _____

5. It is called a pride of <u>lions</u>.   _____

6. A <u>colony</u> of ants can ruin a picnic.   _____

7. A band of <u>gorillas</u> doesn't play marching songs. _____

8. A <u>child</u> may welcome a kindle of kittens.   _____

9. But they will grow into a clutter of <u>cats</u>.   _____

10. Have you seen a covey of quail take to the <u>sky</u>? _____

PART II Write a sentence with the plural form of each word given. (Score: 14—1 for each plural form and 1 for each sentence)

Example:

leaf   *I'll sweep the leaves off the sidewalk later.*_____

11. shelf   _____

12. party   _____

13. key   _____

14. fish   _____

15. woman   _____

16. foot   _____

17. class   _____

LESSON 49
Using Went *and* Gone

> **Handbook Guide 16**
>
> *Went* needs no helping word. *Gone* must have a helping word.

Fill each blank with *went* or *gone*. (Score: 18)

A Visit to Poland

1.   Aunt Mary has _____ on a very special vacation trip.

2.   She has _____ to visit her relatives in northern Poland.

3.   The flight from Chicago _____ over the North Pole.

4.   Aunt Mary had been _____ from Poland for sixty years.

5.   What thoughts must have _____ through her head when the plane landed!

6.   Aunt Mary's sister _____ by train to meet her.

7.   The two sisters must have _____ wild when they saw each other.

8.   They _____ to a cousin's apartment for dinner that first night.

9.   The next day they _____ south by train to my aunt's sister's farm.

10. Aunt Mary _____ through the village where she had grown up.

11. Some of the buildings she remembered were _____.

12. My aunt _____ around hugging her sister's grandchildren.

13. Then she _____ right out and began chopping wood!

14. Last week the family _____ to Zakopane, a village in the Tatra Mountains.

15. According to Friday's postcard they _____ to a dance there.

16. At the dance Aunt Mary met someone she had _____ to school with.

17. My aunt has now been _____ for six weeks.

18. I know she's glad that she _____ on this trip.

Name That Job _____

Decide what occupation the person who uses these things probably has. Then write a paragraph telling how each item is used.

altimeter   throttle   control yoke   radar

Name_____ Perfect Score 28   My Score _____

LESSON 50
Using Flew and Flown

Handbook Guide 16

Flew needs no helping word. *Flown* must have a helping word.

In each sentence, draw a line under the appropriate word in parentheses. (Score: 28)

1. Jean-Pierre Blanchard (flew, flown) in a balloon from Philadelphia to Woodbury, New Jersey, in 1793.

2. No person had (flew, flown) in the United States before then.

3. People in France had (flew, flown) in balloons during the 1780s.

4. In 1852 Henri Giffard (flew, flown) a steam-engine-powered balloon.

5. He (flew, flown) an airship that was 144 feet long.

6. Giffard's airship was not (flew, flown) at a high speed.

7. He (flew, flown) at a speed of about six miles an hour.

8. Archer King and William Black (flew, flown) a balloon over Boston in 1860.

9. They took photographs of the city as they (flew, flown).

10. A gas-engine-powered airship was (flew, flown) in 1872.

11. Could a balloon be (flew, flown) across the Atlantic Ocean?

12. In 1873 a huge balloon was made, but it was never (flew, flown).

13. The balloon ripped before it could be (flew, flown).

14. In 1900 Count Ferdinand von Zeppelin (flew, flown) the first of his airships.

15. These huge, rigid-frame balloons were (flew, flown) for forty years.

16. When was the first airplane (flew, flown)?

17. The Wright brothers (flew, flown) the first airplane on December 17, 1903.

18. Four flights were (flew, flown) that day.

19. A number of women pilots (flew, flown) in those rickety early planes.

20. In 1911 Harriet Quimby first (flew, flown) as a licensed pilot.

21. The first flight across the Atlantic Ocean was (flew, flown) in 1919.

22. In 1927 Charles Lindbergh (flew, flown) solo to Paris.

23. Many daring flights were (flew, flown) by Amelia Earhart.

24. She (flew, flown) solo across the Atlantic Ocean in 1932.

25. Before 1933 no one had (flew, flown) solo around the world.

26. Then Wiley Post (flew, flown) around the world in eight days.

27. Jet planes have been (flew, flown) at speeds of more than 2,000 mph.

28. Today dozens of jets are (flew, flown) across the Atlantic every day.

Name _____   Perfect Score 26   My Score _____

LESSON 51
Writing Words
in Alphabetical Order

Handbook Guide 40

In the box below is a list of words to be arranged in alphabetical order. First, look through the list carefully for a word beginning with *a*. Write it in the first blank. Now find a word beginning with *b*. Write it in the second blank. Continue in this way with the other letters of the alphabet. (Score: 26)

Example:

funny	drop	1.	*ask*	4.	*drop*
bake	every	2.	*bake*	5.	*every*
ask	cold	3.	*cold*	6.	*funny*

call	zebra	mat	value	union
dog	hammer	wagon	quail	pepper
ball	egg	ink	gate	
apple	jay	red	soot	
open	X-ray	town	your	
leaf	friend	name	key	

1. _____   14. _____
2. _____   15. _____
3. _____   16. _____
4. _____   17. _____
5. _____   18. _____
6. _____   19. _____
7. _____   20. _____
8. _____   21. _____
9. _____   22. _____
10. _____   23. _____
11. _____   24. _____
12. _____   25. _____
13. _____   26. _____

Name_____   Perfect Score 24   My Score _____

LESSON 52
Writing More Words in Alphabetical Order

Handbook Guide 40

PART I The words below have been arranged alphabetically to the first letter. In the blanks, arrange the words to the second letter. (Score: 12)

Example:

elm	frog	1. _____eat_____	5. _____fill_____
ever	fold	2. _____elm_____	6. _____fold_____
eat	full	3. _____end_____	7. _____frog_____
end	fill	4. _____ever_____	8. _____full_____

alligator	bug	dream	help
Africa	bad	halt	lug
berry	door	hot	log

1. _____   7. _____

2. _____   8. _____

3. _____   9. _____

4. _____   10. _____

5. _____   11. _____

6. _____   12. _____

PART II Arrange the following words in alphabetical order to the second letter. (Score: 12)

school	leave	bomb	saw
able	cool	noise	two
apple	carpet	bang	three

13. _____   19. _____

14. _____   20. _____

15. _____   21. _____

16. _____   22. _____

17. _____   23. _____

18. _____   24. _____

LESSON 53
Choosing Standard Forms

Draw a line under the appropriate word or words in parentheses. (Score: 24)

Paka, Super Typhoon

1. On December 17, 1997, (a, an) huge typhoon hit the island of Guam.

2. (Can, May) typhoons cause great destruction?

3. Winds (has, have) been clocked at more than 200 miles per hour during typhoons.

4. Typhoon Paka (was, were) the strongest storm of any kind ever recorded.

5. The National Weather Service in Honolulu reported (a, an) wind gust of 236 miles per hour.

6. This (is, are) the fastest wind speed ever measured on Earth.

7. (Wasn't, Weren't) a wind speed of 231 miles per hour recorded on Mount Washington, New Hampshire, in 1934?

8. Yes, but Typhoon Paka (has, have) broken that old record.

9. Guam's residents (wasn't, weren't) prepared for (a, an) storm of such strength.

10. Islanders (saw, seen) trees uprooted and homes flattened.

11. Tin roofs (flown, flew) by as if they were sheets of cardboard.

12. The typhoon (went, gone) on for 12 hours.

13. Amazingly, no deaths (was, were) reported from the storm.

14. However, most of the island's buildings (was, were) either damaged or destroyed.

15. Trees had (fall, fallen) over, knocking power lines to the ground.

16. Red Cross workers from the continental United States hurried (two, to, too) Guam.

17. They said they had never (seen, saw) such widespread damage.

18. President Bill Clinton declared Guam (a, an) federal disaster area.

19. Guam received money from the United States government to help (it's, its) people make repairs.

20. (Isn't, Aren't) a typhoon similar to a hurricane?

21. Yes, (there, they're) both tropical storms.

22. Paka (has, have) been classified as (a, an) super typhoon—the most intense of all tropical cyclones.

Connecting Meanings _____

Draw a line from each word in row 1 to its meaning in row 2. Then write a sentence using each word in row 1.

Row 1	define	refine	confine
Row 2	make purer	keep in a small place	explain the meaning of

Name_____

LESSON 54
Writing a Summary

Read a Summary of a News Article

When you retell just the most important facts in a news article, you create a **summary** of it. Knowing how to write a summary can help you communicate information quickly and clearly.

Here are some tips for writing a summary of a news story:

- The summary should be much shorter than the original story. It should include only the **most important information**. For example, *Who* is the story about? *Where* and *when* does it take place? *What* happened? *Why* or *how* did it happen?

- Give the names of the real places and people mentioned in the article.

- Help the reader understand the **order of events** by using words such as *first*, *then*, and *next*.

- Begin a new paragraph whenever you begin talking about a different idea or a different time.

The following paragraphs are a summary of a newspaper article that appeared in the *San Francisco Chronicle* on March 16, 1998. Read the summary.

Help Slow in Coming for Flood Victims

In February 1998 it rained hard in California for weeks. After especially heavy rains, the White River in California's Central Valley surged over its banks. Hundreds of homes in the small town of Earlimart were flooded. The water stayed high for days. Houses and belongings were ruined. The government promised to give the people of Earlimart money for repairs. One month later, the money still has not come.

Today, homes in Earlimart are dirty and smelly from polluted mud still inside them. Many people cannot go back to their homes yet. The people of Earlimart are angry and frustrated. They want to know when the money will come. Some local people think that because Earlimart is a small farming town, the government doesn't care much about it. The reporter who wrote this article has called government agencies to try to find out why they haven't helped. So far, he hasn't found any answers.

Complete these items about the summary above.

1. *Where* does the story take place? _____

_____

2. *When* does it take place? _____

_____

Underline all the words that tell when. Include dates and words that describe the passing of time.

3. *Who* are the important people in the story? _____

_____

4. *What* happened to them? _____

_____

5. *Why* are the people upset now? _____

_____

6. *How* could their problem be solved? _____

_____

7. How many paragraphs does this summary contain? _____

_____

8. The writer began a new paragraph because of a change in _____.
   a. idea   b. time   c. speaker

9. One of the families whose home was flooded has a son named Ramón. Is this important information to include in the summary? Why or why not? _____

_____

Write a Summary of a News Article

Read the front page articles of a newspaper. Pick one news story and write a summary of it.

1. **Plan**

   Use this space to plan your summary. Write the most important facts on the lines below. Leave out details that don't have to do with the main story.

   Where? _____

   When? _____

   Who? _____

   What? _____

   Why or How?_____

2. **Write**

   Now write your summary on another piece of paper. Use your notes to guide you.

3. **Reread and Correct**

   Reread your summary. Does it include all the important information? Does it answer the questions *who*, *where*, *when*, *what*, and *why*? Have you started a new paragraph with each change of idea or change in time? Have you spelled all the place names correctly? Make any necessary corrections. You can make a clean copy of your corrected summary if you like.

Name_____   Perfect Score 50   My Score _____

LESSON 55
Unit V Review

1. Write a sentence that begins with a quotation. Then   **Handbook Guide 8**
    write the same sentence with the quotation at the end.
    (Score: 2)

    _____

    _____

2. After each pair of words listed, give the singular and   **Handbook Guide 14**
    plural of another word that forms its plural in the
    same way. (Score: 12)

    cat, cats   _____   woman, women   _____

    elf, elves   _____   chimney, chimneys   _____

    baby, babies   _____   dish, dishes   _____

3. Write four sentences, using one of the words at the   **Handbook Guide 16**
    left in each sentence. (Score: 4)

    went   _____

    gone   _____

    flew   _____

    flown   _____

4. Write the alphabet. Then write words that fit in   **Handbook Guide 40**
    alphabetical order between the words given in each
    group below. (Score: 34)

    ___ ___ ___ ___ ___ ___ ___ ___ ___ ___ ___ ___ ___

    ___ ___ ___ ___ ___ ___ ___ ___ ___ ___ ___ ___ ___

    bat _____ bill _____ bump   fall _____ fed _____ fuss

    ham _____ hid _____ hum   take _____ tell _____ tub

LESSON 56
Dividing Words

Handbook Guide 41

When it is necessary to divide a word at the end of a line, divide it only at the end of a syllable. Most dictionaries show how to divide words.

PART I   Draw a vertical line between the two syllables of each of the following words. Use a dictionary to help you. (Score: 27)

Example:

to | day

1.	rabbit	10.	dishes	19.	lifted
2.	winter	11.	blister	20.	forward
3.	skimming	12.	pretty	21.	taxes
4.	father	13.	seven	22.	misses
5.	flower	14.	turtle	23.	farmer
6.	river	15.	until	24.	mountain
7.	spoken	16.	window	25.	sorry
8.	winner	17.	pinecone	26.	pupil
9.	Sunday	18.	nineteen	27.	unpaid

PART II   Divide each of the following words into syllables. Place hyphens between the syllables. Do not divide a word of one syllable. (Score: 20)

Examples:

boy   _____*boy*_____   butterfly   _____*but-ter-fly*_____

28.	younger	_____	38.	crazy	_____
29.	ageless	_____	39.	lake	_____
30.	aid	_____	40.	frighten	_____
31.	barrel	_____	41.	cabbage	_____
32.	answer	_____	42.	without	_____
33.	morning	_____	43.	accident	_____
34.	summer	_____	44.	unhappy	_____
35.	birthday	_____	45.	carrying	_____
36.	wood	_____	46.	valentine	_____
37.	quarter	_____	47.	suddenly	_____

Name_____   Perfect Score 40   My Score _____

LESSON 57
Sticking to the Paragraph Topic

Handbook Guide 18

In writing a paragraph, it is important to stick to the topic, or subject.

Each paragraph below is about a separate topic, but some sentences in the paragraphs do not stick to the topics. Draw a line through each sentence that has nothing to do with the topic, or subject, of its paragraph. (Score: 5 for each sentence that does not belong; you should find eight in all)

1. Bora Bora is one of the most beautiful islands in the world. It lies in the South Pacific Ocean, not far from Tahiti. I enjoy reading books about travel. The mountains of Bora Bora are covered with bright green forests. The island is protected by a coral reef. Many people are afraid of sharks. Bora Bora is truly a paradise.

2. The space shuttle is an important step in space exploration. Many people hope to visit the moon. We need spacecraft that can return to Earth and be used again. With the space shuttle we can build and maintain space stations. We also might use the shuttle to transport people to the moon and distant planets. Jupiter is the largest planet in the solar system. I would rather visit Mars, though. The space shuttle program is expensive, but it is a needed step in the conquest of space.

3. Will women baseball players someday play in the major leagues? Baseball fans have strong opinions on the subject. I enjoy playing football and volleyball. Some fans think that women are not strong enough to compete with men in professional ball. Others think that skill and dedication are more important than strength. Ken Griffey, Jr., and Greg Maddux are two of the greatest baseball players of the modern age. They are my favorite players. Most fans, however, would probably be quick to applaud any skillful player—man or woman.

Odd Word Out _____

Circle the word in this list that does not belong with the others. Name a category that would fit the four uncircled words. Then name a category for the word you circled.

spare   strike   gutter   rebound   frame

LESSON 58
Combining Sentences

Combine these short, choppy sentences into smoother, more interesting ones. (Score: 20—10 for each part)

1. Camille runs a school. It is a dog-training school. People bring their dogs there. They bring them to obedience classes. Camille works with the dogs. She works with their owners. At the end of the course the owners are happy. They are happy to be able to control their pets. The dogs are happy. They are happy to be able to please their owners.

_____

_____

_____

_____

_____

_____

_____

_____

2. The old trapper climbed up. He climbed to the top of the ridge. He looked down. A forest of trees stretched before him. They were pine trees. He wanted to cross the forest. He wanted to do this by nightfall. But he had a long way to go. He lifted his pack to his shoulders. He started down the path. It was rocky.

_____

_____

_____

_____

_____

_____

_____

_____

Name_____   Perfect Score 18   My Score _____

LESSON 59
Avoiding Too Many Ands

Handbook Guide 18b, 18c

Rewrite the following paragraphs to avoid unnecessary use of the word *and*. You will then have paragraphs with several shorter and clearer sentences instead of one long, confusing sentence. Divide each paragraph into three sentences. (Score: 18—3 for each sentence)

1.   Learning to ride a skateboard takes skill and practice and the rider must be able to stay balanced and steer the board as it moves and the rider must also be looking ahead to keep from running into things.

_____

_____

_____

_____

_____

_____

2.   The rider pushes with one foot to get the board moving, and steers by shifting weight to one side or the other and the rider can even do tricks such as riding backward and flipping the board up in the air and landing on it and there is always the idea in the rider's mind that more difficult tricks are possible.

_____

_____

_____

_____

_____

_____

Odd Word Out _____

Circle the word in this list that does not belong with the others. Name a category that would fit the three uncircled words. Then name a category for the word you circled.

maneuver   navigate   steer   fumigate

Name_____ Perfect Score 16   My Score _____

LESSON 60
Finding Synonyms

Use this list of words to find a synonym for each italicized word in the sentences below.
Write the synonym in the blank space after the sentence. Use a dictionary for help with word
meanings. (Score: 16)

1. ferocious	5. excellent	9. comical	13. play
2. appear	6. creature	10. ungainly	14. search
3. type	7. however	11. insects	15. tasty
4. huge	8. observed	12. behave	16. darts

Example:

Animals are *interesting*.   *fascinating* _____

1. Each *animal* is suited to its way of life. _____

2. The giraffe's neck helps it reach *succulent* leaves. _____

3. The gnu is an animal with a *funny* name. _____

4. Elephants are *large* animals. _____

5. Sometimes tigers look *fierce*. _____

6. At other times they *frolic* like house cats. _____

7. Ducks are *awkward* on land. _____

8. They are good swimmers, *though*. _____

9. Have you ever *watched* seals in the ocean? _____

10. Seals always *seem* to be enjoying themselves. _____

11. They are *outstanding* divers and swimmers. _____

12. Eagles *look* for food as they fly. _____

13. The butterfly *flits* from flower to flower. _____

14. Bats have a *kind* of natural radar for night flying. _____

15. Most bats feed on either *bugs* or fruit. _____

16. Monkeys and apes sometimes *act* like people. _____

Name_____   Perfect Score 20   My Score _____

LESSON 61
Using Synonyms

In the following sentences, fill each blank with a word that means the same or nearly the same as the word given at the left of the sentence. (Score: 20)

Example:

(jobs) The hotel and food industries offer many good ___*positions*___ .

1.   (amusement) Many people travel for business or _____.

2.   (give) Hotels and motels _____ travelers a place to stay.

3.   (kinds) There are many _____ of jobs in large hotels.

4.   (Perhaps) _____ you should study to be a hotel manager.

5.   (built) Many new hotels and motels have been _____.

6.   (opportunity) You may have a good _____ for a job in this field.

7.   (initial) Many people get their _____ job in the food service industry.

8.   (dining) More and more people are _____ out nowadays.

9.   (aids) This trend _____ restaurants of all kinds.

10.   (running) Have you ever thought about _____ a small business?

11.   (substantial) Many fast-food outlets are making _____ profits.

12.   (make) Profits and growth _____ new jobs.

13.   (skillful) People who are _____ cooks are in demand.

14.   (excellent) Restaurant chefs can earn _____ salaries.

15.   (tedious) Kitchen work in restaurants can be _____.

16.   (wish) Diners _____ to be treated well.

17.   (honor) Waiters and waitresses need to _____ this wish.

18.   (sector) Food packaging is a large _____ of the food industry.

19.   (satisfying) There are many _____ careers in the field of nutrition.

20.   (increasing) In fact, nutrition is a field of _____ importance.

LESSON 62
Choosing Homophones

Draw a line under the appropriate word in parentheses. (Score: 60)

1. We wanted (to, too, two) have a vacation that was not (to, too, two) expensive.

2. We hoped (to, too, two) get away for (to, too, two) weeks.

3. We (knew, new) that some airlines were offering special (knew, new) fares to Hawaii.

4. The fares were (to, too, two) good (to, too, two) pass up.

5. (To, Too, Two) people could fly (to, too, two) Hawaii for the price of one.

6. But we had to (by, buy) our tickets (by, buy) Friday.

7. We visited a travel agency's (knew, new) Web site because we (knew, new) they would have information about Hawaii there.

8. After seeing (their, there) pictures, we could hardly wait to get (their, there).

9. "(You're, Your) sure (you're, your) travel agency can help us?" I asked the agent.

10. "(You're, Your) going to have the time of (you're, your) life!" the agent said.

11. "I (no, know), but (no, know) one will rent me any scuba gear," I answered.

12. We took only (for, four) bags (for, four) the two weeks.

13. Carrying (to, too, two) bags each makes it easier (to, too, two) travel.

14. During (our, hour) flight we watched a film for over an (our, hour).

15. We (eight, ate) dinner at (eight, ate) o'clock that night.

16. We could (sea, see) the lights of Honolulu in the distance across the (sea, see).

17. (There, Their) at the airport many passengers did not get (there, their) luggage.

18. We (new, knew) we had been wise to carry our (new, knew) bags with us.

19. Because traffic was heavy, (our, hour) trip to the hotel took an (our, hour).

20. The next day the sky was (blue, blew), and a breeze (blue, blew) gently.

21. "I hope I can (here, hear) the wind blow through the palms (here, hear)," I said.

22. We hurried (threw, through) the hotel and (threw, through) our gear into the car.

23. We went (to, too, two) a surfing lesson at (to, too, two) o'clock.

24. Neither (one, won) of us (one, won) any prizes for our performance.

25. Later we (road, rode) mountain bikes on a dirt (road, rode).

26. On (to, too, two) of the days we stayed in the sun (to, too, two) long.

27. We decided to (right, write) for the (right, write) directions to get to Kahuku.

28. There the wind (blue, blew) each afternoon, but the (blue, blew) ocean was warm.

29. We tried to (see, sea) the other main islands as we flew across the (see, sea).

30. (No, Know) person I (no, know) likes Hawaii more than I do.

Name_____   Perfect Score 30   My Score _____

LESSON 63
Finding Antonyms

warmer	summer	odd	hill	starting
found	late	backward	old	largest
smooth	top	sunset	tiny	spending
falling	tender	came	pulling	weakest
outside	full	closing	downward	frowned
familiar	happy	straight	ugly	cheap

From the words above, find a word that has the opposite meaning of each word below. Write this antonym in the blank space opposite the word. (Score: 30)

Example:

broad _____*narrow*_____

1. new _____
2. empty _____
3. expensive _____
4. sunrise _____
5. saving _____
6. smiled _____
7. forward _____
8. huge _____
9. opening _____
10. bottom _____
11. early _____
12. upward _____
13. finishing _____
14. cooler _____
15. smallest _____

16. winter _____
17. lost _____
18. strange _____
19. rising _____
20. tough _____
21. strongest _____
22. sad _____
23. went _____
24. valley _____
25. rough _____
26. even _____
27. inside _____
28. handsome _____
29. curly _____
30. pushing _____

Optional Exercise: Write three sentences about two people who are very different from each other. Use a pair of antonyms in each sentence.

LESSON 64
Choosing Standard Forms

Draw a line under the appropriate word in parentheses. (Score: 40)

1.   Jane is (won, one) of the best auto mechanics I (no, know).

2.   Did you (no, know) that she has worked on cars for twelve years?

3.   Her father was (a, an) professional auto mechanic.

4.   As (a, an) child, Jane spent many (ours, hours) watching him work.

5.   At the age of twelve she rebuilt (a, an) old wreck.

6.   Whenever people (through, threw) away useful parts, she retrieved them.

7.   She had (to, too, two) (by, buy) a few parts, (to, too, two).

8.   Within (ate, eight) months she put that car back together.

9.   A neighbor (saw, seen) the car in front of her house.

10. He offered to (by, buy) it for five hundred dollars.

11. Jane didn't (no, know) how to drive a car.

12. She (saw, seen) (no, know) reason to keep the car.

13. (It's, Its) still running.

14. (By, Buy) means of her own skill, Jane had earned some money.

15. She decided (to, too, two) become (a, an) automobile mechanic.

16. She worked on cars every (our, hour) she could spare.

17. Sometimes she wouldn't even (meat, meet) her friends after school.

18. (By, Buy) dinner time she would be covered with grime.

19. She would run home to put some (meat, meet) on bread.

20. She would make (a, an) sandwich or (to, too, two).

21. Then she would run back again to work on (a, an) engine.

22. (By, Buy) the time she was eighteen, Jane was a professional mechanic.

23. "(Can, May) she fix my car?" asked a friend.

24. "Yes, and you (can, may) ask her now," I answered.

25. "(Is, Are) you sure?" my friend said.

26. Jane (saw, seen) the problem within (a, an) (our, hour).

27. "(It's, Its) a tough problem, but I'll fix it," Jane said.

28. The next day my friend (went, gone) to get the car.

29. Now (it's, its) engine purrs like a kitten.

30. Jane has (a, an) interesting job and (a, an) bright future.

Name_____

LESSON 65
Writing a Descriptive Paragraph

Read a Descriptive Paragraph

When you write to tell what a person, place, or thing is like, you are creating a description. Here are some guidelines for writing a descriptive paragraph:

- Begin your paragraph with a topic sentence that tells what the paragraph will be about.

- In the rest of the paragraph, give several supporting details that tell more about the topic.

- Try to use colorful words and phrases that appeal to the five senses: sight, hearing, taste, smell, touch.

- Tell how you feel about what you are describing.

Read this example of a descriptive paragraph:

A Walk Through Chinatown

Taking a walk through New York's Chinatown district is like visiting a far-away Asian city. Sidewalk markets are crowded with shoppers. People are buying bok choy, foot-long green beans, dried squid, and other delicacies. Dark, slippery fish wiggle in shallow seawater. The sweet, smoky smell of roasting ducks drifts from restaurants. A visit to Chinatown during the Lunar New Year offers even more wonderful and unusual sights. You might see dancers dressed as huge, colorful lions making their way down the narrow streets. You might hear drums and firecrackers accompany the dancers as they bring greetings of good luck to the storekeepers. The Lunar New Year is the most exciting time of the year for a visit, but a walk through Chinatown on any day will make you feel like you've traveled around the world and back.

Complete these items about the descriptive paragraph above.

1. What is the topic of this paragraph?_____

2. Which sentence tells what the whole paragraph is about? Underline it.

3. Where in the paragraph does this sentence appear? _____

4. The author has used many details to give readers a feeling for what New York's Chinatown is like. Reread the paragraph. Look for details that appeal to the five senses: *sight*, *hearing*, *taste*, *touch*, and *smell*. Write some details the author has used on the lines below.

   sight _____

   smell_____

   sound _____

5. How does the author seem to feel about a visit to Chinatown? How can you tell?

_____

_____

6. Find a descriptive detail that you think is especially effective. Write that detail here.

_____

_____

Write a Descriptive Paragraph

Think of a place you would like to visit with a group of your friends. Pick a place you like a lot and know well. Write a descriptive paragraph about that place. You can use the paragraph on page 74 as a model.

1.   Plan

Use this space to plan your descriptive paragraph. In the middle of the web, write the name of the place you want to write about. In the outside circles, list some details that appeal to the five senses.

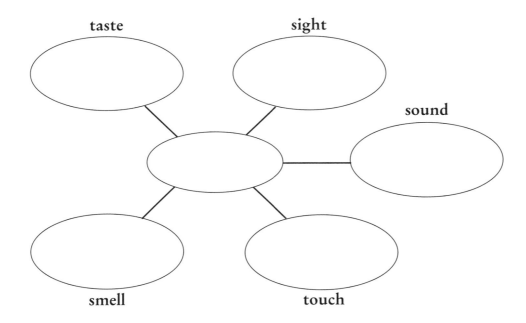

2.   Write

Write your description on another piece of paper. Use your notes in the web to guide you.

3.   Reread and Correct

Now reread your paragraph. Look for mistakes in spelling. Look up any words you're not sure of. Also make sure that your paragraph has a topic sentence. Then make corrections. If you want, you can make a clean copy of your corrected paragraph.

Name_____   Perfect Score 24   My Score _____

LESSON 66
Unit VI Review

1. Write three words that have two syllables and place a | Handbook Guide 41 |
    hyphen between the syllables of each word. (Score: 3)

    _____   _____   _____

2. Which two rules for writing paragraphs do you think | Handbook Guide 18a |
    are most important? Write them. (Score: 2)

    _____

    _____

3. Write two short sentences describing an animal. Then | Handbook Guide 18b |
    combine these two sentences into one longer sentence.
    (Score: 3)

    _____

    _____

    _____

4. Write four pairs of synonyms. (Score: 4) | Handbook Guide 34 |

    a. _____ _____   c. _____ _____

    b. _____ _____   d. _____ _____

5. Write four pairs of antonyms. (Score: 4) | Handbook Guide 35 |

    a. _____ _____   c. _____ _____

    b. _____ _____   d. _____ _____

6. Use *a* and *an* in the same sentence. (Score: 2) | Handbook Guide 29 |

    _____

7. For each pair of homophones below, write a sentence | Handbook Guide 33 |
    in which you use both homophones correctly. (Score: 6)

    a. threw, through   _____

    b. no, know   _____

    c. your, you're   _____

Name_____ Perfect Score 20   My Score _____

UNIT
VII

LESSON 67
Using Has *and* Have

Use the word *has* when speaking of one person or thing. Use *have* when speaking of more than one person or thing. Always use *have* with *you* or *I*.

PART I In the following sentences, fill each blank with *has* or *have*. (Score: 14)

1. Mary, Beth, and I _____ hiked at high altitudes in North America.

2. We _____ hopes of exploring ancient ruins in Peru.

3. _____ you read about the Incas?

4. Beth _____ studied the history of Peru.

5. She _____ always wanted to visit South America.

6. We _____ been studying Spanish to prepare for our travels.

7. I _____ read about the old Inca cities.

8. We _____ now reached the city of Cuzco.

9. This city _____ thin air because it is at an elevation of 11,024 feet above sea level.

10. It _____ a population of nearly 255,000 people.

11. Mary, Beth, and I _____ our tickets and backpacks here with us.

12. We _____ to travel seventy miles north of Cuzco to reach Machu Picchu.

13. That city _____ been known as the last hiding place of the Incas.

14. Since 1911, tourists _____ been able to visit the city.

PART II Draw a line under *has* or *have*. (Score: 6)

15. Mary (has, have) climbed a hill to get a better view.

16. Machu Picchu today (has, have) only the remains of its great stone buildings.

17. Green vegetation (has, have) covered the stone in many places.

18. The Peruvians (has, have) built a comfortable inn.

19. Mary and Beth (has, have) decided to explore the ruins.

20. We (has, have) never seen a more impressive sight.

Name_____   Perfect Score 23   My Score _____

LESSON 68
Learning to Use Troublesome Contractions

> **Handbook Guide 28**
>
> Use *hasn't* and *doesn't* when speaking of one person or thing. Use *haven't* and *don't* when speaking of more than one person or thing. Use *haven't* and *don't* with *you* or *I*.

Draw a line under the appropriate word in parentheses. (Score: 23)

Finding Information

1. I (don't, doesn't) know where I can find information on the 1998 Olympic Winter Games.

2. (Haven't, Hasn't) you looked in an encyclopedia?

3. Our library (don't, doesn't) have any encyclopedias new enough to include that information.

4. (Haven't, Hasn't) you got any other suggestions for me?

5. (Don't, Doesn't) the library offer access to the Internet?

6. I (don't, doesn't) know, since I (haven't, hasn't) asked about it.

7. You probably (hasn't, haven't) visited the PBS Web site for the 1998 Olympics.

8. No, I (haven't, hasn't).

9. You probably (haven't, hasn't) looked in the *Reader's Guide to Periodical Literature* either.

10. *The Reader's Guide to Periodical Literature* lists recent magazine articles, (don't, doesn't) it?

11. (Don't, Doesn't) this issue of *Sports Illustrated* have the information you need?

12. It (don't, doesn't) seem to have any articles about bobsled races.

13. It (haven't, hasn't) any articles about luge events either.

14. (Don't, Doesn't) the *Reader's Guide* list any articles about speed skating?

15. (Haven't, Hasn't) you heard of Bonnie Blair, who won gold medals in 1988, 1992, and 1996?

16. She has retired from competition, (haven't, hasn't) she?

17. (Don't, Doesn't) this almanac list all the gold medalists in recent Olympic games?

18. You have to find articles about new Olympic champions, (don't, doesn't) you?

19. I (haven't, hasn't) decided whether to write about an event or a person.

20. (Don't, Doesn't) this article about downhill skiing look interesting?

21. I (haven't, hasn't) been able to choose a topic for my report yet.

22. (Haven't, Hasn't) you ever had this problem?

Odd Word Out _____

Circle the word in this list that does not belong with the others. Name a category that would fit the four uncircled words. Then name a category for the word you circled.

trestle   naval   nautical   vessel   port

LESSON 69
Using Contractions

PART I   In each blank, write the contraction of the words in parentheses. (Score: 17)

1.   (do not) Often timid people _____ enjoy parties.

2.   (it is) Sometimes _____ hard to have fun with a group of people.

3.   (Has not) _____ everyone felt awkward at a party now and then?

4.   (You will) _____ have to find a way to begin having fun.

5.   (cannot) You _____ expect someone else to take the first step.

6.   (Could not) _____ you just start talking to people near you?

7.   (They are) _____ probably as uncomfortable as you are.

8.   (They will) _____ be glad that you started a conversation.

9.   (Is not) _____ a question a good way to begin a conversation?

10. (I am) _____ sure that people enjoy being asked about themselves.

11. (should not) You _____ do all the talking.

12. (you are) Soon you will find that _____ having fun.

13. (Did not) _____ your new friends have some interesting opinions?

14. (Have not) _____ some of you seen the same movie?

15. (Was not) _____ that a funny story someone told?

16. (That is) _____ a story to remember.

17. (Will not) _____ it be a good story to tell to a new acquaintance?

PART II   Write a sentence with the contraction of each pair of words below. (Score: 5)

18. had not   _____

19. are not   _____

20. that is   _____

21. I have   _____

22. we are   _____

Name_____   Perfect Score 30   My Score _____

LESSON 70
Using I *and* Me

> **Handbook Guides 17f, 17g, 25**
>
> Use *I* as the subject of a sentence. Use *me* after words of action, such as *give*, *see*, and *tell*, and after such words as *to*, *for*, *with*, and *from*.
>
> Always place the word *I* or the word *me* last when you write about yourself and others in the same sentence.

PART I   Fill in the blank spaces in each sentence below with the word *I* and the word or words in parentheses. Be sure that the word *I* is placed in its standard position. (Score: 11)

Example:

(Tom, Betty) _____*Tom*_____, _____*Betty*_____, and _____*I*_____ play in a jazz band.

1. (Betty) _____ and _____ started the band.

2. (she) _____ and _____ had been practicing together.

3. (Judy) _____ and _____ both play saxophone.

4. (Tom, Judy) _____, _____, and _____ practice every day.

5. (Tom) _____ and _____ need more practice.

PART II   Fill in the blank spaces with the word *me* and the word or words in parentheses. (Score: 11)

6. (Terri) Some friends helped _____ and _____ paint the house.

7. (Bob) Terri gave _____ and _____ the paint for the bedroom.

8. (Ling) Later she moved _____ and _____ to the kitchen.

9. (Bob, Ling) Susan poured lemonade for _____, _____, and _____.

10. (them) Someone left a surprise gift for _____ and _____.

PART III   Fill in the blank spaces with *I* or *me*. (Score: 8)

11. Please give _____ the history book.

12. _____ want to read about ancient Athens.

13. Tom gave Bob and _____ some souvenirs.

14. Terri and _____ want to visit Greece.

15. She and _____ will eat Greek food.

16. Nikos taught _____ a Greek dance.

17. He and _____ have packed our suitcases.

18. Will you give him and _____ a ride to the airport?

Name_____   Perfect Score 26   My Score _____

LESSON 71
Using Come *and* Came

Handbook Guide 16
Came needs no helping word. *Come* is usually used with a helping word.

PART I   Fill each blank with *came* or *come*. (Score: 16)

1.   Paul's grandfather _____ to the United States in 1918.

2.   He had _____ from Poland.

3.   Paul's grandmother _____ from Germany.

4.   She had _____ to live with her sister.

5.   Paul's grandfather _____ to the town where she lived.

6.   No one guessed that they would _____ to marry each other.

7.   "Will you _____ with me to Texas?" he asked.

8.   "Yes, I will _____ with you," she answered.

9.   After a few years in Texas, they _____ to southern California.

10. They met friends who had _____ from Mexico.

11. The Espinoza family _____ from Guadalajara.

12. Many families from Mexico have _____ to southern California.

13. Maria Espinoza _____ to Los Angeles last fall to study medicine.

14. I _____ to Los Angeles to study chemistry.

15. Maria and I have _____ to be good friends.

16. Both our families have _____ to visit us.

PART II   Write five sentences about a family's life in the United States. Use the words in parentheses. (Score: 10—2 for each sentence)

17. (came)   _____

18. (had come)   _____

19. (came)   _____

20. (has come)   _____

21. (have come) _____

Name_____   Perfect Score 19   My Score _____

LESSON 72
Using Took and Taken

Handbook Guide 16

Took needs no helping word. *Taken* must always have a helping word.

Fill each blank with *took* or *taken*. (Score: 19)

1. I _____ a trip to Paris last year.

2. I have _____ many trips to France.

3. Some of my business trips have _____ me to strange places.

4. Once, a group of us _____ a boat up the Amazon River.

5. Our leader had _____ many trips to Brazil.

6. We _____ lots of insect repellent with us.

7. I have never _____ a more exciting voyage.

8. We have always _____ pictures of the places we visit.

9. The pictures we _____ in Brazil were very unusual.

10. We had _____ them for magazines in the United States.

11. After visiting Paris, I _____ a week off to go skiing.

12. Three of us _____ the morning train for Switzerland.

13. "Have you _____ your ski equipment?" someone asked.

14. "Yes, I've _____ everything I need," I answered.

15. Because of heavy snow, the train _____ a long time to get there.

16. We _____ a rest before going out on the mountain.

17. One skier had _____ a spill down the slope.

18. We _____ her to the first aid center.

19. I _____ a picture of her after she had been bandaged.

Connecting Meanings

Draw a line from each word in row 1 to its meaning in row 2. Then write sentences using each word in row 1.

Row 1	traverse	travel	travail
Row 2	to journey	hard labor	to cross

LESSON 73
Learning to Use Homophones

PART I Fill each blank space with *to, too,* or *two.* (Score: 15)

1. Last winter we took a trip _____ New York City.

2. We spent _____ weeks going from place _____ place.

3. It was really _____ cold to do much walking.

4. The _____ of us were not going _____ let the cold keep us indoors.

5. First, we went _____ the Radio City area.

6. We had _____ walk down Broadway, _____.

7. There were _____ museums I had _____ see.

8. We went _____ the American Museum of Natural History.

9. Then we walked _____ the zoo in Central Park.

10. We spent _____ days at the Metropolitan Museum of Art.

11. It was a thrill _____ see New York City from the top of the Empire State Building.

PART II Fill each blank with the appropriate word—*their* or *there.* (Score: 11)

12. Cesar and Nora took _____ family to Mexico City.

13. _____ Cesar found a good job.

14. Nora took care of _____ three children.

15. _____ children liked living _____.

16. When all the children were in school, _____ was time for Nora to work.

17. She went to see a businesswoman who knew _____ families.

18. The woman remembered _____ parents and friends.

19. Nora found a job _____ with no trouble at all.

20. Now _____ income is higher.

21. Cesar and Nora can move _____ family into a larger house.

Optional Exercise: Use *to, two, too, their,* and *there* in written sentences.

Name_____ Perfect Score 36 My Score _____

LESSON 74
Learning to Use Commas

Place commas where they are needed in these sentences. (Score: 36)

Handbook Guides 8c, 10-12

Commas are used to separate certain words and phrases in sentences. When the word *yes* or *no* is used to begin a sentence that answers a question, place a comma after it.

Examples:

Yes, I saw the game.

No, I was not at Tom's house.

"*Yes,* Juan, I like soccer, tennis, and swimming," answered Les.

Game Time

1. "Did you see the soccer game yesterday Roberto?"

2. "Yes Susan" answered Roberto. "Did you see it?"

3. "No I was playing tennis."

4. "Did you play singles Susan?"

5. "No I played doubles with María Max and Tom."

6. "Roberto would you like to go to a baseball game this afternoon?"

7. "Yes let's join the others and go together."

8. Susan Roberto María and Max went to the ball game together.

9. They sang songs whistled and told stories as they rode to the park.

10. "Did you remember to bring everything Max?" asked Susan.

11. "Yes I did. The food the napkins and the seat cushions are in the trunk."

12. Cars trucks buses and even campers were parked around the stadium.

13. "Have you ever seen such a crowd María?"

14. "Yes I saw a huge crowd in Bogotá at a soccer match," she replied.

15. "Roberto do you remember how excited the fans were?"

16. "Yes María. We thought they wouldn't stay in the stands."

17. María Max and Susan found their seats while Roberto parked the car.

18. María and Max watched as the players stretched jogged and played catch.

19. They ate sandwiches pickles boiled eggs and ice cream.

20. The home team scored one run in the first inning two in the second and one in the third.

21. Susan said "Isn't this an exciting game Max?"

22. "Yes Susan. It's the best game we've seen all year."

LESSON 75
Choosing Verb Forms

Draw a line under the appropriate word in parentheses. (Score: 28)

Seeing America

1.   Millions of tourists (have, has) visited the Grand Canyon.

2.   This beautiful canyon (was, were) carved by the Colorado River.

3.   The walls of the canyon (is, are) beautiful in the sunlight.

4.   Have you ever (saw, seen) the huge coast redwoods in California?

5.   I (saw, seen) the Golden Gate Bridge when I visited San Francisco.

6.   California (has, have) many kinds of climate and scenery.

7.   My brother has (saw, seen) Carlsbad Caverns in New Mexico.

8.   (Has, Have) you ever (saw, seen) the bats in these caverns?

9.   Carlsbad Caverns National Park (was, were) established in 1930.

10.   The Cave of the Winds in Colorado (is, are) beautiful, too.

11.   (Isn't, Aren't) you going to see the Garden of the Gods?

12.   The huge, oddly shaped stones (make, makes) us feel that we are in a fairyland.

13.   Many people (write, writes) of the wonders of Yellowstone Park.

14.   Most of this national park (is, are) in the state of Wyoming.

15.   No one (is, are) allowed to harm the wild animals in any national park.

16.   (Doesn't, Don't) rangers enforce the rules in national parks?

17.   The rangers (take, takes) care of the trees and other plants, too.

18.   Many people have (came, come) to fish in the large lake.

19.   Wise tourists (doesn't, don't) ever leave food in their cars.

20.   Bears have often (went, gone) into cars to find food.

21.   At sunset we (saw, seen) bears come from the forest to look for food.

22.   All the trash cans (has, have) chains on them to keep the bears out.

23.   We (seen, saw) Old Faithful spout high into the air.

24.   The water in that pond (is, are) very blue.

25.   (Weren't, Wasn't) you surprised to see snow in August in Yellowstone Park?

26.   The Rocky Mountains in Yellowstone (is, are) very beautiful.

27.   There (is, are) even a colorful pool of boiling clay in Yellowstone.

Name_____

LESSON 76
Writing a Persuasive Paragraph
Read a Persuasive Paragraph

Handbook Guide 18a

To write a persuasive paragraph, start by stating your opinion. Then give reasons for your opinion, and use words to appeal to the reader's emotions. Finally, tell readers what they can do to help.

When you write to try to convince people to agree with you about something, you create a persuasive paragraph. Here are some tips for writing a persuasive paragraph.

- State your **opinion** in the first sentence of the paragraph.
- In the body of the paragraph, give **reasons** why you feel as you do. Give at least three reasons. Don't repeat the reasons more than once.
- You may also want to use **emotional words** that will affect your readers' feelings. *Unjust, outrageous,* and *victorious* are examples of emotional words.
- In the last sentence, give a **call to action**. Tell your readers what they can do!

Read this example of a persuasive paragraph:

Why the New Curfew Is a Bad Idea

In my opinion, the new 11:00 p.m. curfew for teenagers 18 years old and under is unfair. First of all, this new law unjustly labels teenagers as wrongdoers. The law makes it seem as if most nighttime crimes and traffic accidents are caused by teenagers. If you read the crime reports, though, you will see that most of the late-night crimes are committed by adults. Secondly, the law ignores the fact that some teenagers must drive home from work after 11:00 p.m. For example, my cousin Rod works at a restaurant. His Friday night shift doesn't end until 11:30. This law could cause him to lose his job. Finally, this law stops most teenagers from going to movies and concerts that get out after 11:00. Besides being unfair to kids, the curfew hits owners of theaters and other nighttime businesses right in the pocketbook. The leaders who passed the curfew say that its purpose is to keep young people and the community safe. But when you think about it, the curfew doesn't really help anyone. If you agree that the curfew law should be changed, call the members of the city council and tell them exactly how you feel.

Complete these items about the persuasive paragraph above.

1. Underline the sentence that states the writer's **opinion** about the curfew.

2. Where in the paragraph does that sentence appear? _____

3. Put a star by each **reason** the writer gives for her opinion.

4. Circle two **emotional words** the writer has used.

5. What does the writer tell readers to do in the last sentence? _____

_____

6. Why do you think she has included this advice? _____

_____

Write a Persuasive Paragraph

Now you can try your hand at writing a persuasive paragraph. Write about a rule or law you believe is unfair, or a cause you support. Use the model on page 86 as an example.

1. **Plan**

    Write a sentence identifying a rule or law you think should be changed, or a cause you support. Do this on the first line below. On the second line, write a sentence telling what your opinion is.

    rule, law, or cause: _____

    my opinion: _____

    Now give three reasons why you feel as you do. Put the most important reason first.

    1. _____
       _____

    2. _____
       _____

    3. _____
       _____

    Finally, think of something your readers can do to change the rule or law, or to support the cause. Write it here.

    _____
    _____
    _____

2. **Write**

    Write your persuasive paragraph on another piece of paper. Use your notes to guide you. Write with strong feeling—tell your readers why you feel as you do and use language that's powerful enough to convince them! Tell people what they can do to help.

3. **Reread and Correct**

    Reread your paragraph. Have you used emotional words that strengthen your message? Does your last sentence tell readers what they can do to help? Have you spelled every word correctly? Make any needed corrections. If you want to, make a clean copy of your persuasive paragraph.

UNIT VII

LESSON 77
Unit VII Review

1. Form the contractions of the following words.   **Handbook Guide 13**
    (Score: 6)

    they are _____   he is _____   did not _____

    was not _____   are not _____   has not _____

2. Write sentences, using the word at the left of the line   **Handbook Guides 16, 28, 33**
    in each sentence. (Score: 8)

    has   _____

    haven't   _____

    don't   _____

    came   _____

    to   _____

    too   _____

    their   _____

    they're   _____

3. Write a sentence that tells something you and two   **Handbook Guide 12**
    other people did. Use commas where needed. (Score: 2)

    _____

4. Copy these sentences and put in commas where they   **Handbook Guides 8c, 10–12**
    are needed. (Score: 12)

    "Yes you are right Mary," said Esteban.   _____

    _____

    "No Tom the last flight leaves at midnight" Marta explained.   _____

    _____

    Mary said "We are taking sandwiches fruit and milk with us."   _____

    _____

    "Marta Mary and I are each saving twenty dollars" said Tom.   _____

    _____

LESSON 78
Capitalization

Underline each uncapitalized word or initial that should begin with a capital letter. (Score: 75)

Robert E. Lee

1. i have just read the book *the gentleman commander.*

2. it is a story of the life of robert e. lee.

3. when lee was a boy, he lived in alexandria, virginia.

4. in july 1825, lee went to the United States Military Academy at West point.

5. isn't West point in the state of new york?

6. later he became superintendent of the academy at West point.

7. after graduating from this school, lee became a colonel in the united states Army.

8. he was serving in texas when the Civil War started.

9. colonel lee did not wish to fight against either his country or his state.

10. lee was offered command of the Confederate Army.

11. At the same time abraham lincoln asked him to command the Federal Army.

12. at this time col. lee lived in arlington, virginia.

13. he refused to accept a commission until virginia joined the Confederacy.

14. in june 1861, he became commander in chief of the confederate army.

15. lee fought bravely for the South during the civil war.

16. the soldiers loved, admired, and respected him.

17. lee rode a gray horse named traveller.

18. traveller always brought him back safely from scouting.

19. lee was very fond of his horse.

20. the night of july 4, 1863, was a bad one for the Confederates.

21. on that night the city of vicksburg, mississippi, fell to the Federal Army.

22. after the end of the Civil War, lee returned to his home in virginia.

23. later he was asked to be president of washington college.

24. he became president of that school on october 2, 1865.

25. it is called washington and lee university now.

26. lee died on october 12, 1870, at lexington, virginia.

27. he is buried in a chapel on the school campus.

28. thousands of people visit the chapel each year.

LESSON 79
Punctuation

Handbook Guides 7, 8, 10–13, 17c–e

In the following sentences, place punctuation marks where they are needed. (Score: 70)

1. Have you heard of Tara VanDerveer

2. Shes one of the worlds most successful basketball coaches

3. She was head coach of the USA Olympic Women's Basketball Team in 1996

4. Didnt the womens team capture the gold medal that year

5. VanDerveer is smart experienced and firm

6. Did she ever play basketball herself

7. Yes she played guard on the Indiana University womens varsity team

8. Then she served as women's basketball coach at Ohio State University the University of Idaho and Stanford University

9. Wasnt she named Coach of the Year in womens college basketball

10. Yes this honor was given to VanDerveer in 1988 1989 and 1992

11. The Stanford womens basketball team won championships in 1990 and 1992 under her guidance

12. Hasnt Tara VanDerveer coached in other countries, too

13. Yes she has coached American women's teams in England Brazil Australia and Russia

14. For many years women had no opportunity to play professional basketball in the United States

15. In 1996 a new professional league for women, the American Basketball League, began play

16. Didnt several players whom VanDerveer coached at Stanford join ABL teams

17. Yes Jennifer Azzi Sonja Henning and Anita Kaplan all became San Jose Lasers

18. In 1996 the Women's National Basketball Association (WNBA) was also formed

19. Eight cities were given teams in the new league

20. These included Phoenix Los Angeles Cleveland and Houston

21. The first WNBA season began in June of 1997

22. The WNBA doesnt play during winter like the NBA and the ABL.

23. The founders of the WNBA believe that a summer season will draw larger audiences

24. Do you think Tara VanDerveer will ever coach a professional team Shana asked

25. Well thats hard to say Gwen replied

26. Im a big fan of the Stanford Cardinal she continued

27. I hope VanDerveer continues to coach that team for many years she said

LESSON 80
Using **We** *and* **Us**

Handbook Guides 17f, 17g, 26

Use *we* **as the subject of a sentence. Use** *us* **after words of action, such as** *give,* **see, and** *tell,* **and after such words as** *to, for,* **with, and** *from.*

In the following sentences, fill each blank with *we* or *us.* (Score: 21)

A Year without Rain

1. _____ look up at the sky.

2. The clear blue sky does not please _____.

3. _____ see no sign of rain.

4. All the land around _____ is brown and thirsty.

5. This summer _____ are suffering through a drought.

6. _____ see field after field of dying crops.

7. None of _____ can enjoy these sunny days.

8. _____ usually grow large amounts of wheat.

9. Some of _____ grew up during the 1930s.

10. Because of that fact, _____ know all about dust storms.

11. Bone-dry soil is nothing new to _____.

12. _____ are afraid of the wind, for good reason.

13. All of _____ know how wind blows dusty soil away.

14. One person showed _____ a sad sight.

15. _____ saw how the wind had harmed the young wheat.

16. People in cities and suburbs depend on _____.

17. Usually _____ supply tons of wheat for bread.

18. But this is a hard year for _____.

19. Soon _____ must finish our study and write a report.

20. The report from _____ will give a gloomy picture.

21. _____ hope the rains come and wash away all our notes.

Name_____   Perfect Score 22   My Score _____

LESSON 81
Forming Possessives

PART I   Write the possessive form of each of the following words. (Score: 10)

Examples:

Robert   *Robert's*   women   *women's*   girls   *girls'*

1.	dogs	_____	6.	friend	_____
2.	men	_____	7.	calf	_____
3.	clock	_____	8.	Mary	_____
4.	mouse	_____	9.	birds	_____
5.	Charles	_____	10.	mice	_____

PART II   In each blank space, write the possessive form of the word at the left. (Score: 12)

11.   (car) The _____ windshield was covered with ice.

12.   (women) The _____ voices sounded worried, and the men were pale.

13.   (Joan) _____ sister had forgotten to buy gas.

14.   (school) The _____ parking lot was almost empty.

15.   (people) These _____ plans did not include a walk in the snow.

16.   (passengers) Suddenly the _____ hearts began to thump.

17.   (wolf) They thought they heard a _____ howl.

18.   (train) But it was only a _____ whistle.

19.   (driver) The _____ hand turned the key.

20.   (engine) The _____ roar made everyone feel warmer.

21.   (children) They drove past some _____ snow forts.

22.   (station) A gas _____ sign was a welcome sight.

Synonym Watch _____

Circle a word in the second row that is a synonym of a word in the first row. Draw a line to connect it to its synonym.

Row 1	precipitation	precipice	precise
Row 2	real	rain	ruin

LESSON 82
Using Negatives

Handbook Guide 36

Rewrite the following sentences, removing words to correct the double negatives. Be careful. Some sentences do not need to be changed. Copy any sentence that does not need to be changed. Watch capitalization and punctuation. (Score 9)

Example:

She didn't have no time to look up the correct answer. *She didn't have time to look up the correct answer.*

An Eight-Armed Enemy

1. The diver hadn't seen no danger there among the rocks. _____

2. Hadn't nobody explained that an octopus can change color? _____

3. The octopus didn't give no warning before it grabbed the diver. _____

4. The diver said, "No octopus has ever hurt nobody." _____

5. Hadn't the diver ever fought an octopus? _____

6. "I haven't nothing to worry about," thought the diver. _____

7. Suddenly the diver couldn't see nothing. _____

8. It's not easy to see through octopus ink. _____

9. Escape from those eight arms was not hardly easy. _____

LESSON 83
Avoiding Unnecessary Words

Draw a line through the unnecessary word or words in each sentence. Write the deleted word or words in the blank after each sentence. (Score: 38—2 for each sentence)

Example:

The peace officer ~~she~~ waved to Tim.   *she*_____

The Rustlers

1. "Where are you going to?" Tim asked the officer.   _____

2. She replied, "I'll be driving along that there dirt road."   _____

3. "I have got to catch some rustlers," she continued.   _____

4. "Are rustlers operating in this here county?" asked Tim.   _____

5. The officer said, "Yes, we have like a real problem."   _____

6. The officer went and started her car.   _____

7. "Would you like to come on this here search?" asked the officer.   _____

8. Tim he replied, "Yes, I sure would."   _____

9. "Well, let's try to like find that there bunch," said the officer. _____

10. The officer wasn't sure where the rustlers were at.   _____

11. The officer and Tim they kept looking out across the desert.   _____

12. Suddenly Tim said, "I see something on that there mesa!"   _____

13. "We have got to be careful," said the officer.   _____

14. "Where are the cattle at?" asked Tim.   _____

15. "These here rustlers aren't cattle rustlers," she said.   _____

16. The officer she continued, "These are cactus rustlers."   _____

17. "They steal these here cactuses from our state park," she said.   _____

18. The rustlers' hands were like bleeding from the cactus stickers.   _____

19. "We've gone and caught them red-handed!" said Tim.   _____

LESSON 84
Spelling Synonyms

Here are some words you should know how to spell. Can you spell them?

chief	remember	stared	invite	afraid
quiet	loud	received	talking	dismiss
dirty	house	beautiful	worried	operate
extremely	pleased	examine	answer	assist

From the list of words above, choose a synonym for the italicized word in each sentence below. Write the synonym in the blank. (Score: 20)

1. Captain Omo walked over to the *main* advisor.   _____

2. "You must *help* me," she said to him.   _____

3. "I will be *speaking* with Commander Glim," she added.   _____

4. The advisor remained *silent.*   _____

5. Captain Omo said, "I must visit the commander at her *home.*"   _____

6. The advisor said, "She was *very* upset after seeing your ship."   _____

7. "But our ship is a *lovely* ship," said Captain Omo.   _____

8. "It was quite *filthy* when she saw it," the advisor said.   _____

9. "And its engine was *noisy,*" continued the advisor.   _____

10. "Did she *inspect* it last night?" asked the captain.   _____

11. "Yes, but I haven't *gotten* her report," said the advisor.   _____

12. "Do you *recall* when the commander departed?" asked Captain Omo.   _____

13. The advisor did not *reply.*   _____

14. The captain became *concerned.*   _____

15. "Will she *fire* me?" asked Captain Omo.   _____

16. Captain Omo *looked* at the advisor intently.   _____

17. "You need not be *scared* of that," said the advisor.   _____

18. "Then why would she *ask* me to meet with her?" asked the captain.   _____

19. "You are to *drive* the new Space Turtle," said the advisor.   _____

20. Was Captain Omo *glad* to hear this?   _____

UNIT VIII

LESSON 85
Using Himself *and* Themselves

Handbook Guide 27

PART I   Draw a line under the appropriate word in parentheses. (Score: 12)

1. Who calls (himself, hisself) the man in black?

2. Johnny Cash sings of good-hearted people who respect (themselves, theirselves).

3. Johnny (himself, hisself) was one of seven children.

4. The Cash family had to work hard to keep (themselves, theirselves) fed.

5. They often sang hymns and folk songs to keep (themselves, theirselves) happy.

6. Did Johnny learn to play the guitar by (himself, hisself)?

7. Cash made (himself, hisself) famous with such songs as "Ring of Fire."

8. Many singers try to make (themselves, theirselves) sound like someone else.

9. But Johnny Cash has always sounded like (himself, hisself).

10. Singers often find (themselves, theirselves) quickly forgotten.

11. Cash (himself, hisself) has been popular for more than forty years.

12. Even when things were not going well, he did not let (himself, hisself) be defeated.

PART II   Write *himself* or *themselves* in each blank below. (Score: 10)

13. Singers often dress _____ in colorful clothes.

14. But Johnny Cash usually dresses _____ in black.

15. He wrote a song about _____ called "Man in Black."

16. Johnny Cash made _____ into a great entertainer.

17. Johnny has sung by _____ and also with his wife, June Carter.

18. June Carter and her sisters were famous singers _____.

19. Is it important for people to respect _____?

20. Johnny Cash _____ seems to say so in his songs.

21. He _____ is proud of his Cherokee ancestors.

22. Cash has sung of Native Americans who have brought _____ glory.

Antonym Watch _____

Circle a word in the second row that is an antonym of a word in the first row. Then draw a line connecting the two words.

Row 1	ancestors	prospectors	promoters
Row 2	delinquents	descendants	dependents

LESSON 86
Choosing Standard Forms

Draw a line under the appropriate word in parentheses. (Score: 35)

Superstitions

1. (We, Us) may think of superstitions as things of the past.
2. These beliefs (began, begun) many years ago, but many still exist today.
3. (Are, Is) there many forms of superstitions?
4. Horseshoes (are, is) thought to be good-luck charms.
5. People who fear Friday the thirteenth (is, are) superstitious.
6. (Is, Are) the number thirteen an unlucky number?
7. Magnets (were, was) once believed to be able to heal people.
8. Some said that sickness could be healed (buy, by) eating walnuts.
9. Others said you would be healed if you (drank, drunk) special potions.
10. Patients (was, were) sometimes helped because of their faith in these methods.
11. Will bad luck come (to, too, two) someone who spills salt?
12. If your (right, write) or left ear burns, is someone talking about you?
13. (Its, It's) believed by some that a sneeze is a bad omen.
14. (We, Us) old-timers know several superstitions about animals.
15. If (an, a) groundhog sees its shadow on February 2, winter will last six more weeks.
16. Black cats (are, is) signs of bad luck, according to old beliefs.
17. A rabbit's foot (are, is) a good-luck charm.
18. Some people believe that (there, their) actions can cause good or bad luck.
19. (To, Too, Two) begin a trip on a Friday is bad luck, (for, four) example.
20. Some believe that knocking on (wood, would) can drive bad luck away.
21. Many people are (taught, learned) that breaking a mirror is bad luck.
22. Does dropping (a, an) knife or fork mean guests (is, are) coming over?
23. Are you (one, won) who believes that it is bad luck to walk under a ladder?
24. Would you become ill if you (drunk, drank) milk after you (ate, eaten) fish?
25. Superstitions are (not, knot) new.
26. Many superstitions have (to, too, two) do with important events in life.
27. Parents once believed that if (their, they're) children (was, were) born on Sunday, they would always have good luck.
28. Scientists (theirselves, themselves) may be superstitious about some things.
29. Haven't you (never, ever) (took, taken) a walk around a ladder?
30. Have you ever (broke, broken) a mirror and then worried about bad luck?

LESSON 87
Using the Writing Process to Write a Personal Narrative

Handbook Guides 18, 21

Personal narratives are written in the first-person voice.

Read a Personal Narrative

When you write to tell about an experience in your life, you create a **personal narrative**. Writing about personal experiences can help you preserve and share important moments. Writers usually use the first-person voice when writing about themselves and their experiences. Here are some guidelines for writing an effective personal narrative:

- Tell about events using the **first-person voice**: use the pronouns *I*, *me*, *mine*, and *my*.
- Make sure your narrative has a **beginning**, a **middle**, and an **end**.
- Be sure to tell **where** and **when** the events happened.
- Help the reader understand **the order in which the events took place** by using words such as *first*, *next*, *then*, and *finally*.
- Describe your **feelings** as well as your **actions**. Use colorful adjectives and expressive adverbs.
- Use **conversational language**, including informal expressions and contractions, so your narrative sounds as if you are speaking to the reader.

Read this example of a personal narrative:

The Hike

Last summer our youth group planned a hiking trip in the Mission Mountains, near our home in Missoula, Montana. We were supposed to hike six miles, eat lunch, and then hike back. When my mom asked me to take my little brother Deke along, I wasn't happy. It's bad enough having to share a room with someone six years younger. I couldn't believe I'd have to take him with me on the trip.

The hike started out okay. When the trail started getting steep, Grady, Stu, and I fell behind. Of course, Deke hung around us the whole time, like a mosquito you can't get rid of. We rested awhile and then went on, but pretty soon we came to a fork in the trail. "Which way did they go?" Grady asked. We yelled for the others, but it was no use. They were too far ahead.

Stu said, "Let's try this way." We took the left fork. It led up a hill and into a thick grove of trees. The trail got more and more faint, and then it just disappeared. We kept going to the top of the hill, figuring we could see the group from up there. When we got to the top, there was nothing but ridge after ridge of dark forest in every direction. We decided to turn around, pick up our trail, and just go back to the van. But we couldn't even find the trail. After hiking for an hour, we passed the same gnarled tree root. At that point we had to admit we were lost.

"I have an idea," Deke said. I told him to keep his mouth shut and stay close. "No, I really have a good idea," he said, digging deep into the front pocket of his jeans. He pulled out two things—a whistle and a compass. We followed Deke then. He stopped a lot to check the compass. We took turns blowing the whistle, which really was loud—lots louder than we could yell. It was late afternoon by the time we got back to the van. The others were already there, waiting for us. I don't know what would have happened if Deke hadn't been with us that day. I do know that on the next trip, I'll be the one who invites Deke to come along.

Complete these items about the personal narrative on page 98.

1.   Find a sentence that shows the writer is using the **first-person voice**. Circle a personal pronoun in it that refers to the writer.

2.   Put a star by a paragraph that begins with a **change of speaker**.

3.   What does the writer tell the reader at the **beginning** of this narrative?

   _____

4.   What does he describe in the **middle** of the narrative?

   _____

5.   How does he **end** the narrative?

   _____

6.   Underline two words that help tell the order in which events happened.

7.   Circle one detail that shows how the narrator felt about his brother at the beginning of the story. Draw a box around one detail that shows how he felt at the end of the story.

8.   Put a star by a sentence that is a good example of the use of **conversational language**.

Write a Personal Narrative

Now you'll have a chance to write a personal narrative of your own. In your narrative, tell about an experience you had that was important for some reason. You can use the narrative on page 98 as a model.

   I.   Prewriting

      1. **Choose a Topic.** On another piece of paper, write down two or three first-time experiences you might like to write about. Circle the idea you like best.

      2. **Think About Sequence.** Write down the events you will tell about, in the order they happened.

   II.   **Write a First Draft**. Using your notes to help you, write a first draft on another piece of paper. Write your first draft quickly. Just try to get all your ideas down. Don't worry about spelling. You will have a chance to fix any errors later.

   III.   **Revise**. Read over your first draft. Ask yourself these questions:

      Does my narrative have a beginning, a middle, and an end?
      Have I written in the first person, referring to myself as *I*?
      Have I told my readers when and where the action takes place?
      Have I told readers how I felt during this experience?
      Is the order of events clear?
      Have I started a new paragraph with every change of idea, time, place, or speaker?

   Now make the changes.

   IV.   **Proofread**. Read over your revised narrative carefully. Look for errors in spelling, punctuation, and capitalization.

   V.   **Publish**. Make a clean copy of your personal narrative. Write it by hand, or type it using a word processor. Then share your narrative with a friend or family member.

Name_____ Perfect Score 30 My Score _____

LESSON 88
Unit VIII Review

1. Rewrite the following sentences, adding necessary
    capitalization and punctuation. (Score: 13)

    Handbook Guides 1, 10–12, 17c, 17d

    in august, will irma go to troy, ohio _____

    _____

    yes elsa the car has a heater a cellular phone and a CD player _____

    _____

2. Write the possessive forms of these words. (Score: 6) Handbook Guide 15

    daisy_____ daisies _____ men _____

    Tess _____ players _____ calf _____

3. Rewrite the following sentences. Correct double
    negatives and take out unnecessary words. (Score: 3)

    Handbook Guides 26, 36, 37

    She hadn't never said nothing unkind. _____

    _____

    Us riders don't hardly have a chance to win. _____

    _____

    Where is my book at? _____

    _____

4. Write sentences, using the word at the left in each.
    (Score: 8)

    Handbook Guides 27, 33

    himself   _____

    themselves   _____

    ate   _____

    to   _____

    too   _____

    two   _____

    hear   _____

    here   _____

LESSON 89
Reviewing Sentences

PART I For each sentence fragment in Section A, find a group of words in Section B that will combine with it to form a complete sentence. Write the complete sentences on the lines below. Be sure to capitalize and punctuate carefully. (Score: 10—2 for each sentence)

Section A

when the umpire yelled, "Play ball!",
the pitcher's wild curve ball
the runner on third
because the manager argued,
with the bases loaded,
hitting a home run

Section B

the umpire became angry
dashed toward home plate
the game began
hit the batter
made Becky the hero
Becky hit the ball deep

Example:

When the umpire yelled, "Play ball!", the game began. (first line of Section A and third line of Section B)

1. _____

_____

2. _____

_____

3. _____

_____

4. _____

_____

5. _____

_____

PART II Write *yes* before each group of words that is a complete sentence. Write *no* before each incomplete sentence. Punctuate the sentences. (Score: 12—2 for each numbered item)

_____   6. As soon as the game is over   _____   9. The batter struck out

_____   7. Did someone steal home   _____   10. An error in the third inning

_____   8. the player broke the bat   _____   11. Running to home plate

Name_____ Perfect Score 33   My Score _____

LESSON 90
Reviewing Standard Forms

Handbook Guides 16, 28, 30, 33

Draw a line under the appropriate word in parentheses. (Score: 33)

Libraries

1. Andrew Carnegie (did, done) much for libraries.

2. He (gave, given) over sixty million dollars to libraries in the United States.

3. (Is, Are) he the one who worked in a cotton mill when he was young?

4. He worked as a bobbin boy for (won, one) dollar and twenty cents a week.

5. Andrew (knew, new) that books (is, are) very helpful to people who want to learn.

6. (Wasn't, Weren't) the first circulating library in (hour, our) nation established (by, buy) Benjamin Franklin?

7. (Isn't, Aren't) the New York Public Library the largest free public library on the East Coast?

8. (Whose, Who's) going (there, their, they're) this summer?

9. The Library of Congress in Washington, D.C., (is, are) the largest library in the world.

10. Do you (no, know) which public library is the largest in the United States?

11. (It's, Its) the (one, won) in Chicago known as the Harold Washington Library Center.

12. Long ago people (wrote, written) on the skins of animals, on tablets of clay, and on blocks of wood.

13. The Egyptians learned how (to, too, two) make paper from papyrus.

14. (Doesn't, Don't) the papyrus reed grow on the banks of the Nile River?

15. Parchment (is, are) writing material made from the skins of sheep and goats.

16. Didn't the early people of Western Asia (right, write) on clay tablets?

17. Only a few people in ancient times (was, were) able (to, too, two) read.

18. Now there (is, are) several thousand public libraries in our country.

19. (Hour, Our) public libraries serve people almost everywhere in the nation.

20. Books have been (took, taken) to remote places in bookmobiles.

21. Books in Braille (is, are) lent (to, too, two) people who are blind.

22. (Isn't, Aren't) these books written with raised dots for letters?

23. People who know Braille (can, may) read these books easily.

24. (Isn't, Aren't) books on tape available for borrowing, (to, too, two)?

25. These recordings let people (here, hear) great books read aloud.

LESSON 91
Reviewing More Standard Forms

Handbook Guides 16, 28–30, 33, 36

Draw a line under the appropriate word in parentheses. (Score: 35)

A Dangerous Place to Fly

1. Bolivia is (a, an) small country in South America.

2. (Its, It's) western section includes part of the Andes Mountains.

3. Most of this part of Bolivia (is, are) over (to, too, two) miles high.

4. Pilots flying in this area risk (their, they're, there) lives.

5. Beef must be (flew, flown) from the ranches to the city of La Paz.

6. Older airplanes (is, are) used for most of these flights.

7. These old planes cannot be (flew, flown) over the mountains.

8. They must be (took, taken) through the mountain passes.

9. Pilots (no, know) that (one, won) mistake can result in a crash.

10. (There, Their, They're) very brave to fly between mountains.

11. (There, Their, They're) planes are tossed about (by, buy) shifting winds.

12. There aren't (any, no) weather stations.

13. Mountains can't be (saw, seen) through storm clouds.

14. (Aren't, Isn't) La Paz the capital of Bolivia?

15. La Paz (is, are) the highest major city in the world.

16. (It's, Its) 11,910 feet above (see, sea) level.

17. More than 976,000 people live (here, hear) in La Paz.

18. Plane accidents (is, are) more common in this area than in other places.

19. Those metal street signs (was, were) molded from wrecked planes.

20. The tales of the pilots will make (your, you're) heart skip a beat.

21. One pilot found (himself, hisself) heading for (to, too, two) mountain peaks.

22. His plane's engines (wasn't, weren't) working.

23. He put the plane into (a, an) vertical bank to miss them.

24. The plane felt like it would shake (to, too, two) pieces.

25. The plane hit the top of (one, won) of the peaks and bounced right off.

26. The pilot (flew, flown) down through the mountains without (no, any) power.

27. The plane was going almost 400 miles an (our, hour).

28. Then the engines suddenly (began, begun) to work again.

29. (Can, May) you believe that?

Name_____ Perfect Score 86   My Score _____

LESSON 92
Reviewing Punctuation and Capitalization

In the following sentences, supply the missing punctuation marks and draw a line under each uncapitalized word that should begin with a capital letter. (Score: 86)

1. gold was discovered in the foothills of california in 1848
2. what happened when people heard the news
3. san francisco san diego and monterey were soon almost deserted.
4. Did people from New England immediately rush to California?
5. No people there werent very excited.
6. Then president james k polk made a speech.
7. President Polks speech informed americans of the discovery of gold.
8. What huge fortunes can be made! a man shouted.
9. "Perhaps i will soon be rich" he thought.
10. Ships sailed around south america to San Francisco California.
11. One ship left New York on january 18 1849
12. It arrived Monday August 6 1849
13. Usually the ships were crowded dirty and dangerous
14. Some people went through panama to the pacific ocean.
15. The sixty-mile trip often took from monday until friday.
16. Many travelers died of yellow fever malaria or other diseases.
17. Some travelers headed for the West in covered wagons
18. the wagon trains were troubled by sickness heat and breakdowns.
19. "I've counted eighty-five dead animals in one mile" exclaimed one traveler.
20. Alicia asked, Did some people become rich during the Gold Rush
21. "well alicia some did make large fortunes" mr henry said.
22. Then the stories weve heard are true, Alicia replied
23. Thousands who made the trip ended up with nothing" mr henry said
24. You should read the story 'The luck of roaring camp,' continued mr henry
25. "Was that story written by bret harte?" alicia asked

Name That Job _____

Decide what occupation the person who uses these things probably has. Then write a paragraph telling how each item is used.

stethoscope   thermometer   otoscope   tongue depressor

Name_____ Perfect Score 30 My Score _____

UNIT IX

LESSON 93
Reviewing Synonyms and Antonyms

Handbook Guides 34, 35, 40

raise	reply	ill	error	above
certain	shut	help	bright	little

PART I From the list of words given above, choose a word that means the same or nearly the same as each of the words given below. Write this synonym in the blank space opposite each word. (Score: 10)

1. lift _____
2. close _____
3. shiny _____
4. aid _____
5. over _____

6. sure _____
7. answer _____
8. mistake _____
9. sick _____
10. small _____

backward	warmer	falling	pulling	ugly
straight	happy	tender	frowned	shiny

PART II From the list of words above, choose a word that has the opposite meaning of each word listed below. Write this antonym in the blank space opposite each word. (Score: 10)

11. pushing _____
12. dull _____
13. smiled _____
14. rising _____
15. forward _____

16. sad _____
17. cooler _____
18. tough _____
19. handsome _____
20. curly _____

PART III Arrange the numbered words in Part II in alphabetical order on the blank lines below. (Score: 10)

21. _____
22. _____
23. _____
24. _____
25. _____

26. _____
27. _____
28. _____
29. _____
30. _____

Name_____   Perfect Score 46   My Score _____

LESSON 94
Reviewing Singular and Plural Words

In the first column of words write the plural form after each singular word. In the second column write the singular form after each plural word. (Score: 46)

1.	book	_____	24.	oranges	_____
2.	apple	_____	25.	tables	_____
3.	nut	_____	26.	tablets	_____
4.	pencil	_____	27.	canes	_____
5.	match	_____	28.	flowers	_____
6.	box	_____	29.	marches	_____
7.	brush	_____	30.	squashes	_____
8.	dish	_____	31.	peaches	_____
9.	notch	_____	32.	foxes	_____
10.	church	_____	33.	crutches	_____
11.	man	_____	34.	men	_____
12.	woman	_____	35.	teeth	_____
13.	ax	_____	36.	geese	_____
14.	child	_____	37.	mice	_____
15.	foot	_____	38.	knives	_____
16.	life	_____	39.	loaves	_____
17.	wife	_____	40.	shelves	_____
18.	thief	_____	41.	leaves	_____
19.	wolf	_____	42.	puppies	_____
20.	butterfly	_____	43.	babies	_____
21.	navy	_____	44.	lilies	_____
22.	berry	_____	45.	valleys	_____
23.	boy	_____	46.	days	_____

LESSON 95
Reviewing Possessives
and Contractions

Handbook Guides 13, 15

PART I   Write the possessive form of each of the following words. (Score 22)

1.   man   _____
2.   boy   _____
3.   girl   _____
4.   men   _____
5.   children   _____
6.   mice   _____
7.   James   _____
8.   boys   _____
9.   calf   _____
10. puppy   _____
11. sheep   _____

12. father   _____
13. woman   _____
14. Alice   _____
15. teachers   _____
16. Charles   _____
17. dog   _____
18. kitten   _____
19. Sue   _____
20. child   _____
21. babies   _____
22. cats   _____

PART II   Write the contractions of the following expressions. (Score 22)

23. is not   _____
24. I will   _____
25. you are   _____
26. are not   _____
27. that is   _____
28. does not   _____
29. they have   _____
30. would not   _____
31. were not   _____
32. she is   _____
33. cannot   _____

34. we will   _____
35. they are   _____
36. you will   _____
37. he is   _____
38. we are   _____
39. did not   _____
40. they will   _____
41. you have   _____
42. I am   _____
43. I have   _____
44. was not   _____

Name_____   Perfect Score 36   My Score _____

LESSON 96
Reviewing Uses of a Dictionary

Handbook Guides 40, 41

PART I Rewrite each of these words on the line at the right of the word, placing hyphens between syllables to show places where the word might be divided at the end of a line. Copy any words of one syllable. Use a dictionary for word division, if necessary. (Score: 18)

1. suddenly _____
2. quarter _____
3. unpaid _____
4. mimic _____
5. major _____
6. seven _____
7. forgetful _____
8. lesson _____
9. wagon _____

10. window _____
11. sixteen _____
12. Monday _____
13. pupil _____
14. aid _____
15. blister _____
16. harmful _____
17. turn _____
18. spoken _____

PART II In the spaces below, arrange in alphabetical order the words listed above. (Score: 18)

19. _____
20. _____
21. _____
22. _____
23. _____
24. _____
25. _____
26. _____
27. _____

28. _____
29. _____
30. _____
31. _____
32. _____
33. _____
34. _____
35. _____
36. _____

Word Whiz _____

Use the clues on the left to help you complete the words on the right. Use a dictionary for spelling help.

in ABC order   a __ __ __ __ __ __ i c a l

just a theory   h __ __ __ __ __ __ i c a l

in parentheses   p __ __ __ __ __ __ __ i c a l

Perfect Score 40   My Score _____   **UNIT**
LESSON 97
Reviewing Standard Forms   **IX**

Draw a line under the appropriate word in parentheses. (Score: 40)

1.   (We, Us) painters aren't afraid of high places.

2.   We haven't (ever, never) fallen from a high place.

3.   Yesterday we (went and planned, planned) how to build this scaffold.

4.   Has Cindy (came, come) back from the paint store?

5.   Does she (know, no) where to (meat, meet) us?

6.   She (came, come) back ten minutes ago.

7.   This blue paint is (for, four) the trim.

8.   Last week (there was, there were) ten of (we, us) painters on a job.

9.   (Its, It's) not easy to paint a school auditorium.

10.   "We (haven't any, haven't no) small brushes," said Red.

11.   "(There is, There are) five in my truck," replied Cindy.

12.   (There, Their, They're) is a steep roof on this building.

13.   Which of (we, us) will climb onto the roof?

14.   (Here, Hear) is (a, an) platform to place on the roof.

15.   (Red and I, I and Red) will help Cindy attach it.

16.   (Isn't, Aren't) those (to, too, two) cars traveling (to, too, two) fast?

17.   I just (seen, saw) someone painting stripes on the (rode, road).

18.   I think (its, it's) safer (to, too, two) paint tall buildings.

19.   "(Isn't, Aren't) this (your, you're) scraper?" asked Cindy.

20.   (Don't, Doesn't) the porch steps need to be scraped?

21.   Cindy and Red have stopped to rest (themselves, theirselves).

22.   You must (knot, not) touch this paint because (its, it's) wet.

23.   Never paint (any, no) wall that (has, have) not been cleaned well.

24.   Red just cut (himself, hisself) on the rain gutter.

25.   Yesterday Red and Cindy (ate, eaten) (their, there) lunches in the park.

26.   I (sat, set) here in my truck while I ate.

27.   Then I (sang, sung) along with the radio for five minutes.

28.   (Its, It's) too cold to eat in the park today.

29.   Red and Cindy have made (themselves, theirselves) at home in my truck.

Name_____   Perfect Score 84   My Score _____

LESSON 98
Unit IX Review

PART I   Complete each sentence below. (Score: 24)   Handbook Guides 13, 14, 15, 17a, 29, 30, 33, 34, 35, 40, 41

1.   A sentence expresses a complete _____.

2.   Use *an* before a word beginning with a _____.

3.   Use *a* before a word not beginning with a _____.

4.   Use *may* to ask _____ to do something.

5.   Use *can* to show that you are _____ to do something.

6.   Words that sound alike but are spelled differently and have different meanings are called _____.

7.   Words that have the same meaning are called _____.

8.   Words that have opposite meanings are called _____.

9.   To form the possessive of a plural noun ending in *s*, add _____.

10.   To form the possessive of a plural noun not ending in *s*, add _____.

11.   To form the plurals of most words, add _____.

12.   To form the plural of most words ending in

    (a)   *ch, sh, s, x,* or *z*, add _____.

    (b)   *f*, change the *f* to _____ and add _____.

    (c)   *fe*, change the *fe* to _____ and add _____.

    (d)   *by, dy, ly, my, ny, ry,* or *ty*, change the *y* to _____ and add _____.

    (e)   *ay, ey, oy,* or *uy*, simply add _____.

13.   Only words of at least _____ syllables can be divided at the end of a line.

14.   A word should be divided only between _____.

15.   Words arranged according to the letters in the alphabet are in _____

_____.

16.   Do not confuse *its* with the contraction _____, meaning "it is."

17.   Do not confuse *were* with the contraction _____, meaning "we are."

LESSON 98
Unit IX Review Continued

PART II Underline the appropriate word in parentheses. (Score: 12)   **Handbook Guides 1, 2, 8–13, 15, 17**

18.   Imagine that you have (went, gone) to the moon.

19.   You traveled to the moon (buy, by) space shuttle.

20.   Such rugged mountains are not (saw, seen) on Earth.

21.   (There is, There are) great craters everywhere.

22.   The sky (is, are) black even in daylight.

23.   (There, Their) in the sky is Earth, huge and blue.

24.   Daylight lasts for (to, two too) weeks (hear, here) on the moon.

25.   No plants from Earth (can, may) be grown (hear, here) in the open.

26.   The carrots you (ate, eaten) were grown in that greenhouse.

27.   Most of the food you have (eaten, ate) has been sent here from Earth.

PART III Punctuate these sentences and underline each uncapitalized word or initial that should be capitalized. (Score: 48)   **Handbook Guides 16, 28a, 28c, 30, 33**

28.   on May 5 1961, the United States launched its first rocket with human passengers.

29.   Wasn't the rocket launched from Cape Canaveral Florida

30.   People began thinking about travel to the planets

31.   "lenita do you know what created the craters on the moon?" asked Alba.

32.   I believe they were caused by meteorites Lenita answered.

33.   Alba isnt the daytime temperature on the moon over two hundred degrees Fahrenheit asked lenita.

34.   Yes, but at night it is about two hundred degrees below zero replied Alba.

35.   people on the moon need special suits shoes and helmets said lenita

36.   scientists now believe that there may be water on the moon she continued.

37.   walking on the moon is my number one goal exclaimed tara.

38.   Alba asked "Have you ever read any books by arthur c clarke?"

39.   clarkes books about space travel are exciting she said

THE HANDBOOK

The Guide numbers on the lesson pages refer you to the information given in the following pages. There are forty-two Guides, many of which are divided into sections. The Guides contain rules, explanations, examples, and practice exercises.

Use the Guides whenever you need help with grammar, word use, capitalization, or punctuation. The Guides are listed by topic in alphabetical order at the end of this book.

Capitalization   114

Capitalization with Punctuation   117
   Initials of Names
   Titles with Names
   Names of the Days of the Week
   Names of the Months of the Year
   Addresses
   Titles
   Quotations

Other Uses of Commas   123
   Dates
   Direct Address
   Yes and *No*
   Words in a Series and Two-Part
     Sentences

Contractions   126

Singular and Plural Forms of Nouns   127

Possessive Forms of Nouns   128

Principal Parts of Verbs   129

The Sentence   131

The Paragraph   134

Speaking and Listening   136

The Report   138

The Story   139

The Letter   140
   The Friendly Letter
   The Business Letter
   The Envelope Address
   Postal Code Abbreviations

Troublesome Words   144
   I and *Me*
   We and *Us*
   Himself, Themselves, and *Ourselves*
   Agreement of Verb with Subject
   A and *An*
   May and *Can*
   Teach and *Learn*
   Sit and *Set*

Word Study   150
   Homophones
   Synonyms
   Antonyms
   Double Negatives
   Unnecessary Words
   Expressions to Be Avoided

The Dictionary   155
   Uses of a Dictionary
   Alphabetical Order
   Division of Words
   Spelling

Index of Handbook   158

Capitalization

Guide 1a | **Begin the first word of a sentence with a capital letter.**

She lives in an apartment.

Practice: Rewrite the sentences below; begin each with a capital letter.

1. does the bus stop here? _____

2. there is a fashion show today. _____

3. what a sight that will be! _____

Guide 1b | **Begin each name or nickname of a person or a pet with a capital letter.**

| Eve Marie Myers | Fido | Kitty Gerona |
| Roy Simmons | Uncle George | Mittens |

Practice: Rewrite the following names. Begin each of the names with a capital letter.

1. michael jordan _____ 3. michelle kwan _____

2. oscar wilde _____ 4. pickles _____

Guide 1c | **Begin a person's title before his or her name with a capital letter.**

Mr. Alan Kurtz   Mrs. Pearl Green   Miss Ellen Ott   Ms. Susie Hite

Practice: Rewrite these names. Begin each person's title with a capital letter.

1. mrs. Elena Scio_____ 3. miss Li-Yun Ho_____

2. mr. Donald Helm _____ 4. Ms. Myra Gold _____

Guide 1d | **Write each initial of a name with a capital letter.**

Teresa H. Arana   K. David Selmon   J. R. R. Tolkien

Practice: Rewrite these names. Use a capital letter for each initial of a name.

1. Susan b. Anthony _____ 3. a. b. Dillon _____

2. h. Rider Haggard _____ 4. Sarah e. Fisk _____

Guide 1e | **Capitalize the word *I*.**

I thought I could find a parking space.

Practice: Rewrite the following sentences. Capitalize the word *I*.

1. Jessie and i both play the flute. _____

2. i think i know the answer. _____

Guide 1f | **Begin each word in the name of a particular place or thing with a capital letter.**

Pacific Ocean	Seattle	Deaf Smith County	Kansas Turnpike
Camden Yards	Rio Grande	Cumberland Gap	Lincoln Center
England	Alabama	Mount Hood	Lake Michigan

Practice: Rewrite these names. Use capital letters where they are needed.

1. south africa _____

2. brooklyn bridge _____

3. guthrie theater _____

4. fifth avenue _____

5. snake river _____

6. rocky mountains _____

Guide 1g | **Capitalize a word formed from the name of a place.**

| American | Asian | Swedish | English | Spanish |
| Mexican | African | Australian | Polish | Canadian |

Practice: Rewrite the sentences, capitalizing the words formed from the names of places.

1. Did you know that spaghetti was invented by the chinese and not by the italians? _____

_____

2. Cristina helped build the alaskan pipeline. _____

_____

3. Some hawaiians grow sugarcane. _____

Guide 1h | **Begin the name of a month or a day of the week with a capital letter.**

December   Tuesday

Practice: Rewrite the sentences, capitalizing names of months and days of the week.

1. Your letter arrived thursday. _____

2. Paulo was born in october. _____

3. Do september and april have thirty days each? _____

Guide 1i   Begin the names of holidays and special days with a capital letter.

Easter   Arbor Day   St. Patrick's Day

Do not capitalize the names of the seasons: spring, summer, autumn or fall, winter.

Practice: Rewrite the sentences, capitalizing names of holidays and special days.

1. Mark spent the first day of hanukkah with his uncle. _____

_____

2. Robin always wears red, white, and blue on independence day. _____

_____

Answers to Guide 1 Practice Exercises

Guide 1a

1. Does the bus stop here?
2. There is a fashion show today.
3. What a sight that will be!

Guide 1b

1. Michael Jordan   3. Michelle Kwan
2. Oscar Wilde   4. Pickles

Guide 1c

1. Mrs. Elena Scio   3. Miss Li-yun Ho
2. Mr. Donald Helm   4. Ms. Myra Gold

Guide 1d

1. Susan B. Anthony   3. A. B. Dillon
2. H. Rider Haggard   4. Sarah E. Fisk

Guide 1e

1. Jessie and I both play the flute.
2. I think I know the answer.

Guide 1f

1. South Africa   4. Fifth Avenue
2. Brooklyn Bridge   5. Snake River
3. Guthrie Theater   6. Rocky Mountains

Guide 1g

1. Did you know that spaghetti was invented by the Chinese and not by the Italians?
2. Cristina helped build the Alaskan pipeline.
3. Some Hawaiians grow sugarcane.

Guide 1h

1. Your letter arrived Thursday.
2. Paulo was born in October.
3. Do September and April have thirty days each?

Guide 1i

1. Mark spent the first day of Hanukkah with his uncle.
2. Robin always wears red, white, and blue on Independence Day.

Capitalization with Punctuation
Initials of Names

Guide 2	Write each initial of a name with a capital letter followed by a period.

Herbert George Wells   H. G. Wells

Susan Hope Sax   Susan H. Sax

Charles Abel Allen   C. Abel Allen

When persons have more than one given name, they often use only the initial of one of them when they sign their names. Sometimes they write one given name in full and use the initial of the other.

Practice: Rewrite the following names, using initials for the first and middle names.

1. Arthur Leon Banks   _____

2. Camilo Sandico Calles   _____

Answers to Guide 2 Practice Exercises

1. A. L. Banks   2. C. S. Calles

Titles with Names

Guide 3	Begin a title with a capital letter. Place a period after each title if the title is abbreviated.

Mr. Raymond Best   Miss Marcia L. Frank

Mrs. Alice T. Anderson   Ms. Rachel Fiori

The title used for a man or boy is written *Mr.* The title *Mrs.* is written for a married woman. The title *Miss* is written for an unmarried woman. The title *Ms.* is used for a married or an unmarried woman. The titles *Mr.* and *Mrs.* are abbreviations and are followed by periods. The title *Ms.* is not an abbreviation, but it is usually followed by a period.

A title may indicate the position, rank, or profession of a person. Abbreviations are given in parentheses.

Admiral (Adm.)	Governor (Gov.)	Professor (Prof.)
Colonel (Col.)	Judge (no abbreviation)	Reverend (Rev.)
Doctor (Dr.)	Mayor (no abbreviation)	Senator (Sen.)
General (Gen.)	President (Pres.)	Superintendent (Supt.)

Practice: Fill each blank with an appropriate title, *Mayor* or *Dr.*

1. Tandra has an appointment with her dentist, _____ Mullinix.

2. Now that he has been elected to lead our city, Eileen's father is addressed as

_____ John Gulliver.

Answers to Guide 3 Practice Exercises

1. Dr.   2. Mayor

Names of the Days of the Week

| Guide 4 | Begin the name of each day of the week or its abbreviation with a capital letter. Place a period after each abbreviation shown in parentheses. |

Sunday (Sun.)   Tuesday (Tues.)   Thursday (Thurs.)   Saturday (Sat.)

Monday (Mon.)   Wednesday (Wed.)   Friday (Fri.)

Practice: Write the names of the first four days of the week and the abbreviations for the last three days of the week.

1. _____   5. _____

2. _____   6. _____

3. _____   7. _____

4. _____

Answers to Guide 4 Practice Exercises

1. Sunday   2. Monday   3. Tuesday   4. Wednesday   5. Thurs.   6. Fri.   7. Sat.

Names of the Months of the Year

| Guide 5 | Begin the name of each month of the year or its abbreviation with a capital letter. Place a period after each abbreviation shown in parentheses. |

January (Jan.)   May (no abbreviation)   September (Sept.)

February (Feb.)   June (no abbreviation)   October (Oct.)

March (Mar.)   July (no abbreviation)   November (Nov.)

April (Apr.)   August (Aug.)   December (Dec.)

Note: Do *not* begin the name of a season with a capital letter unless it is the first word in a sentence.

Every *summer* we swim in the lake. (*Summer,* the name of a season, is not capitalized.)

Practice: Write the abbreviations for the months of the year. If a month has no abbreviation, write the full name of the month.

1. _____   5. _____   9. _____

2. _____   6. _____   10. _____

3. _____   7. _____   11. _____

4. _____   8. _____   12. _____

1. Jan.	3. Mar.	5. May	7. July	9. Sept.	11. Nov.
2. Feb.	4. Apr.	6. June	8. Aug.	10. Oct.	12. Dec.

Addresses

Guide 6a   Begin each word in an address with a capital letter. Place a comma between the name of the city and the name or postal code abbreviation of the state.

Prof. Eleanor Wong   Ms. Emma Piper

2206 Bonita Avenue   104 Terrace Drive

Burbank, California 91504   Jackson, MS 39206

An address is the place where a person lives or receives mail. In most mailing addresses, the name of the person is written on the first line, the street address on the second line, and the city, state, and zip code on the third line. When you write an address on an envelope, you must use the correct postal code abbreviation for the state. (See Guide 24.)

Practice: Rewrite this address, using capital letters and punctuation where needed.

1. mrs. elaine spiegle   _____

2. 316 rockaway avenue   _____

3. brooklyn NY 11233   _____

Guide 6b   Capitalize abbreviations used in addresses. Abbreviations made with two capital letters usually are not followed by periods.

E. (East)	S. (South)	Blvd. (Boulevard)	FL (Florida)
W. (West)	SW (Southwest)	Ave. (Avenue)	ME (Maine)
N. (North)	NE (Northeast)	St. (Street)	IL (Illinois)

Abbreviations, short forms of words, save time and space in writing addresses.

Practice: Rewrite the following address, using abbreviations where possible.

1. Mister Rogelio Romero   _____

2. 11 North Alton Street   _____

3. Falmouth, Maine 04105   _____

Guide 6c   When all or part of a person's address is written in a sentence, place commas as follows: after the name of the person, after the street address, after the city, and after the zip code following the state. If the address comes at the end of a sentence, use end punctuation rather than a comma to end the sentence.

Please send a self-addressed envelope to Michelle Pribble, 47 Temple Lane, Princeton, New Jersey 08540, before the end of the month.

Practice: In the sentence below, place commas where they are needed.

1. After checking our records, we found that his address is Mr. Ismail Hager 30 Green Street Dallas Texas 75218.

Answers to Guide 6 Practice Exercises

Guide 6a
1. Mrs. Elaine Spiegle
2. 316 Rockaway Avenue
3. Brooklyn, NY 11233

Guide 6b
1. Mr. R. Romero
   11 N. Alton St.
   Falmouth, ME 04105

Guide 6c
1. After checking our records, we found that his address is Mr. Ismail Hager, 30 Green Street, Dallas, Texas 75218.

Titles

Guide 7a — Capitalize the first word, the last word, and each important word in a title.

Tomás and the Tower Clock   The Night the Ghost Got In

Such words as *a, an, the, of, for, in,* and *to* are usually not capitalized unless they begin or end a title.

Verbs such as *is* and *are* are always capitalized in a title.

Practice: Rewrite these book titles, using capital letters where needed.

1. riders to the sun   _____

2. tomorrow is a new day   _____

3. city daydreams   _____

Guide 7b — Place quotation marks around a title of a story, a poem, or a song when it is part of a sentence. If the title is at the end of a telling sentence, place the end quotation mark outside the period.

One of Dion Henderson's most popular stories is "The Wolf of Thunder Mountain."

Titles of books, movies, TV series, and plays are underlined or printed in italic type when they are used in sentences.

Many science-fiction fans enjoy the old TV series <u>Star Trek</u>. *(underlined)*

OR Many science-fiction fans enjoy the old TV series *Star Trek*. *(italic type)*

Practice: Mark the titles in these sentences.

1. Aaron's favorite television show is Kratt's Creatures.

2. An old railroad engineer sang The Ballad of Casey Jones for us.

Answers to Guide 7 Practice Exercises

Guide 7a

1. Riders to the Sun   2. Tomorrow Is a New Day   3. City Daydreams

Guide 7b

1. Aaron's favorite television show is "Kratt's Creatures."
2. An old railroad engineer sang "The Ballad of Casey Jones" for us.

Quotations

Guide 8a	When using quotation marks to set off someone's exact words in a sentence, begin the quotation with a capital letter.

> The sportscaster shouted, "It's going, going, gone!"

Practice: Underline each uncapitalized word below that should begin with a capital letter.

1. Vicente said, "soccer is a fast-moving game."

2. "how far away is the planet Venus?" asked Anne.

Guide 8b	Enclose the words and punctuation of an exact quotation within quotation marks.

> "I need my glasses only for reading," answered Brett.
>
> Brett answered, "I need my glasses only for reading."

Exact quotations enclosed within quotation marks are direct quotations. Quotation marks are not used with indirect quotations, which are not the speaker's exact words.

> David asked, "Do you have two tickets for the show?" (direct quotation)
>
> David asked whether I had two tickets for the show. (indirect quotation)

Practice: Place quotation marks in these sentences if they are needed.

1. Dawn said, I learned to ski last winter.

2. Dawn said that she learned to ski last winter.

Guide 8c When the speaker's name comes before a direct quotation, place a comma before the beginning quotation marks. When the speaker's name comes after a direct quotation, place a comma, question mark, or exclamation point before the ending quotation marks.

Captain Adams shouted, "Look at that tidal wave!"

"Look at that tidal wave!" Captain Adams shouted.

Remember to enclose both the words and the end punctuation of direct quotations within quotation marks.

Practice: Rewrite and punctuate these sentences.

1. Speed skating is popular in Wisconsin said Lars _____

_____

2. Have you ever seen a sailing ship asked Mariana. _____

_____

3. Felipe said Let's go to the boat show. _____

_____

Answers to Guide 8 Practice Exercises

Guide 8a
1. Vicente said, "soccer is a fast-moving game."
2. "how far away is the planet Venus?" asked Anne.

Guide 8b
1. Dawn said, "I learned to ski last winter."
2. Dawn said that she learned to ski last winter.

Guide 8c
1. "Speed skating is popular in Wisconsin," said Lars.
2. "Have you ever seen a sailing ship?" asked Mariana.
3. Felipe said, "Let's go to the boat show."

Other Uses of Commas
Dates

> **When writing a date, place a comma between the day of the month and the year. Do not place a comma between the name of the month and the year if no day of the month is given.**

December 19, 1998   December 1998

Practice: Place commas where needed in the dates below.

1. September 27 1999   2. April 1988   3. August 1 2012

Guide 9b   **Place a comma between the day of the week and the month.**

Tuesday, June 5   Saturday, October 27

Practice: Place commas in the dates below.

1. Monday May 19   2. Tuesday February 21   3. Sunday November 17

Guide 9c   **When writing a date in a sentence, place a comma after the year unless the year comes at the end of the sentence.**

On *July 20, 1969,* a person first set foot on the moon.

Martin Luther King, Jr., was born on *January 15, 1929.*

Many different items have dates, and it is important for these dates to be written accurately. A newspaper is identified by the month, day, and year it was published. A copyright date on a book shows the year it was published. Very often it is necessary to know exactly when something happened or when something was written. Bills of sale, applications for jobs, contracts, letters, and almost all other written receipts and documents are dated.

Practice: Complete the punctuation of the dates in the sentences below.

1. On July 9 1877 the first telephone company opened for business.
2. The first Super Bowl was won by the Green Bay Packers in January 1967
3. On Sunday January 25 1998 the Denver Broncos won their first Super Bowl.
4. On Nov. 16 1907 Oklahoma became a state.

Answers to Guide 9 Practice Exercises

Guide 9a
1. September 27, 1999
2. April 1988
3. August 1, 2012

Guide 9b
1. Monday, May 19
2. Tuesday, February 21
3. Sunday, November 17

Guide 9c
1. On July 9,1877, the first telephone company opened for business.
2. The first Super Bowl was won by the Green Bay Packers in January 1967.
3. On Sunday, January 25, 1998, the Denver Broncos won their first Super Bowl.
4. On Nov. 16, 1907, Oklahoma became a state.

Direct Address

In writing a sentence, set off the name of the person addressed (direct address) with a comma or commas.

> *Laura,* please open the window.
>
> Did Jesse and I make the team, *Coach?*
>
> Hurry up, *Lester,* or we'll be late.

Notice that only the names used above in direct address are set off with commas.

Practice:　In the sentences below, set off the names in direct address with commas.

1. Jean where are you?

2. I'm over here Felicia behind the screen.

3. Please help me set up the projector Sean.

Answers to Guide 10 Practice Exercises

1. Jean, where are you?
2. I'm over here, Felicia, behind the screen.
3. Please help me set up the projector, Sean.

Yes and No

Guide 11　**When *yes* or *no* is used to begin a sentence that answers a question, place a comma after it.**

> *Yes,* this is the fifth floor.
>
> *No,* the flower shop is not on this floor.

Practice:　Place a comma after *yes* or *no* in the sentences below.

1. Yes I have a library card.

2. No Arabella does not live near the park.

Answers to Guide 11 Practice Exercises

1. Yes, I have a library card.
2. No, Arabella does not live near the park.

Guide 12a	In a series of three or more words, use commas to separate the words. When the last two words are separated by the word *and,* use a comma before the and.

The four seasons are *summer, fall, winter,* and *spring.*

Saturday was a *cold, dark, dreary* day.

Kevin, Rhonda, Doris, and *Paul* will be this year's cheerleaders.

Chico wants us to buy a *loaf of bread, some milk,* and a *chuck roast.*

A word series is a list of three or more words or word groups naming things or persons, or a list of two or more adjectives describing something.

Practice: Use commas where needed to punctuate the series in these sentences.

1. The machine has gears belts and drive wheels.

2. Arizona New Mexico Oklahoma and Texas are southwestern states.

3. Aren't Eloise and Janna sincere faithful friends?

4. The recipe calls for milk a cup of sugar chocolate and nuts.

Guide 12b	When two groups of words that could be separate sentences are joined together by *and,* put a comma before *and.*

Rob made lemonade, *and* Sal baked cookies.

We had a snack, *and* then we went back to work.

Practice: Use commas where needed to punctuate these sentences.

1. The bell rang and the teacher closed the door.

2. I will sweep the floor and you can put away the books.

Answers to Guide 12 Practice Exercises

Guide 12a
1. The machine has gears, belts, and drive wheels.
2. Arizona, New Mexico, Oklahoma, and Texas are southwestern states.
3. Aren't Eloise and Janna sincere, faithful friends?
4. The recipe calls for milk, a cup of sugar, chocolate, and nuts.

Guide 12b
1. The bell rang, and the teacher closed the door.
2. I will sweep the floor, and you can put away the books.

Contractions

Guide 13	In combining two words to form a contraction, use an apostrophe (') to show where letters are left out.

is not	isn't	I am	I'm	he will	he'll
are not	aren't	you are	you're	she will	she'll
was not	wasn't	we are	we're	we will	we'll
were not	weren't	they are	they're	they will	they'll
do not	don't	he is	he's	I have	I've
does not	doesn't	she is	she's	you have	you've
did not	didn't	it is	it's	we have	we've
has not	hasn't	who is	who's	they have	they've
have not	haven't	that is	that's	could not	couldn't
had not	hadn't	I will	I'll	would not	wouldn't
cannot	can't	you will	you'll	should not	shouldn't

The contraction for *will not* is *won't*.

Practice: Write the contraction for each word group listed below. Be sure to place the apostrophe in the appropriate place.

1. they are _____   4. should not _____

2. I will   _____   5. you will _____

3. who is   _____   6. it is   _____

Answers to Guide 13 Practice Exercises

1. they're   2. I'll   3. who's   4. shouldn't   5. you'll   6. it's

Singular and Plural Forms of Nouns

A noun is the name of a person, place, or thing. A noun is singular if it names only one person, place, or thing. It is plural if it names more than one person, place, or thing. The most common way to make a noun plural is to add s to the singular form.

shirt *shirts*   shoe *shoes*   glove *gloves*

The plural forms of some words are written as shown below.

(1) To form the plural of a word ending in *ch, sh, s, x,* or *z,* add *es* to the singular form.

church *churches*   class *classes*   brush *brushes*   ax *axes*

(2) To form the plural of some words ending in *f,* change the *f* to *v* and add *es.*

leaf *leaves*   calf *calves*   thief *thieves*   shelf *shelves*

(3) To form the plural of some words ending in *fe,* change the *fe* to *ve* and add *s.*

life *lives*   knife *knives*   wife *wives*

(4) To form the plural of a word ending in *by, dy, ly, my, ny, ry,* or *ty* (*y* preceded by a consonant letter), change the *y* to *i* and add *es.*

baby *babies*   pony *ponies*   lady *ladies*   cherry *cherries*

lily *lilies*   party *parties*   army *armies*

(5) To form the plural of a word ending in *ay, ey, oy,* or *uy* (*y* preceded by a vowel letter), add *s* in the usual way.

day *days*   monkey *monkeys*   boy *boys*   guy *guys*

(6) To form the plurals of such words as *tooth, man, child, mouse, ox, foot,* and *goose,* change the spelling of the singular form or add a special ending.

tooth *teeth*   man *men*   child *children*   mouse *mice*   ox *oxen*

foot *feet*   goose *geese*

(7) The spelling of some words is the same in both singular and plural form.

deer   sheep   fish (sometimes written *fishes* in the plural)

Practice: Write the plural form of each of these singular words.

1. army _____   4. monkey _____

2. thief _____   5. party _____

3. goose _____   6. ax _____

Answers to Guide 14 Practice Exercises

1. armies   2. thieves   3. geese   4. monkeys   5. parties   6. axes

---

Possessive Forms of Nouns

To form the possessive of a singular noun, add an apostrophe and the letter s ('s).

The *anteater's* nose is very long. *Manny's* home run won the game.

The sentence *That coat belongs to Lois* means that Lois owns or possesses the coat. The sentence can also be written like this: *That is Lois's coat.* Notice how the word *Lois* has been changed to show possession or ownership.

Practice: Read each sentence in parentheses and answer the question after it.

1. (The racer's skis bit into the snow.) Who possesses the skis?   _____

2. (The magician's top hat disappeared.) Who owns the top hat?   _____

3. (The ship's whistle blew.) What does the whistle belong to?   _____

Guide 15b   **To form the possessive of a plural noun that ends in s, add an apostrophe only (').
If the plural does not end in s, add an apostrophe and the letter s ('s).**

The *dancers'* costumes were silver and black.

The *oxen's* hoofprints were easy to see in the mud.

Practice: Write the possessive form of each noun below.

1. classes _____   3. children _____

2. women _____   4. boys _____

Answers to Guide 15 Practice Exercises

Guide 15a
1. the racer   2. the magician   3. the ship
Guide 15b
1. classes'   2. women's   3. children's   4. boys'

Principal Parts of Verbs

Guide 16a   Words that show action, being, or state of being are verbs.

> The runners *entered* the stadium. (action)
>
> Pat Gibbs *is* the chairperson of the committee. (being)
>
> The ocean *seems* calm today. (state of being)

Practice: Underline the verbs in the sentences below.

1. The cafeteria opens at noon.
2. The food is very good.
3. Alfonso was late.

4. He ate his meal quickly.
5. Ethel seemed happy.
6. She wanted two desserts.

Guide 16b   Verbs have three principal parts. blow   blew   blown **The third principal part is often used with one or more of these helping words: *has, have, had, be, is, am, are, was, were, being, been.* These other helping verbs may also be part of the phrase: *shall, will, should, would, could, can, do, did.***

> The wind *blew* hard today. It *has blown* hard for several days.

Study the following principal parts of verbs carefully.

become	became	become	learn	learned	learned
begin	began	begun	ride	rode	ridden
blow	blew	blown	ring	rang	rung
break	broke	broken	rise	rose	risen
bring	brought	brought	run	ran	run
come	came	come	see	saw	seen
do	did	done	set	set	set
drink	drank	drunk	sing	sang	sung
drive	drove	driven	sink	sank	sunk
eat	ate	eaten	sit	sat	sat
fall	fell	fallen	speak	spoke	spoken
fly	flew	flown	swim	swam	swum
freeze	froze	frozen	swing	swung	swung
give	gave	given	take	took	taken
go	went	gone	teach	taught	taught
grow	grew	grown	throw	threw	thrown
know	knew	known	write	wrote	written

Practice: In each sentence underline the appropriate form of the verb in parentheses.

1. Carol (swam, swum) back to shore.

2. She had (took, taken) a long time.

3. I (knew, known) she could do it.

4. She had (broke, broken) the record.

5. I (wrote, written) a story about her.

6. I have (wrote, written) many stories.

Answers to Guide 16 Practice Exercises

Guide 16a

The following words should be underlined:

1. opens   2. is   3. was   4. ate   5. seemed   6. wanted

Guide 16b

The following words should be underlined:

1. swam   2. taken   3. knew   4. broken   5. wrote   6. written

The Sentence

Guide 17a	When you put several words together to express a complete thought, you have made a sentence.

> The pitcher threw a fast ball.
>
> Have you read the newspaper?

The following groups of words are not sentences. They do not express complete thoughts. They leave the reader expecting something else to be added.

> After the plane took off
>
> The first thing I did

Practice: Write *yes* before each group of words that is a sentence and *no* before each group that is not a sentence.

_____   1. Three clouds in the sky.

_____   2. Then everything turned black.

_____   3. When I saw the flash of lightning.

_____   4. The water flooded the street.

Guide 17b	Begin the first word of a sentence with a capital letter.

> The bus stopped for the traffic light.
>
> Where did the bus stop?

Practice: Rewrite these sentences, capitalizing the first word in each one.

1. this restaurant has good food. _____

2. my sister sometimes eats here. _____

Guide 17c	Place a period after a telling sentence. Telling sentences are called *declarative sentences*.

> Linda has a job selling magazines.

Practice: Place the appropriate punctuation after each declarative sentence below.

1. Atlanta is a fast-growing city

2. It is the capital of Georgia

Guide 17d Place a question mark after an asking sentence. Asking sentences are called *interrogative sentences.*

> Did Linda get a new job taking photographs for magazines?

Practice: Place the appropriate punctuation after each interrogative sentence below.

1. Do you know anything about storms

2. What is a tornado

Guide 17e Place an exclamation point after an exclamatory sentence.

> What a great job Linda has!

Practice: Place the appropriate punctuation after each exclamatory sentence below.

1. Oh no, look at all the cars

2. What a horrible traffic jam this is

Guide 17f Every sentence has a subject and a predicate. The subject tells what the sentence is about. The predicate usually tells what the subject did, or what was done to the subject.

> subject   predicate
> The small frog made a loud noise.
> subject   predicate
> Richard was awakened by the noise.

The simple subject is the noun or pronoun that the sentence is about.

> The small *frog* made a loud noise.
> *Richard* was awakened by the noise.
> *I* was awakened, too.

Practice: Underline the simple subject in each sentence.

1. Puffy white clouds drifted across the sky.

2. The two brothers picked strawberries.

3. Susan helped them in the late afternoon.

4. They made strawberry shortcake with the berries.

Guide 17g	The simple predicate is the verb or verb phrase that tells what the subject did, or what was done to the subject.

The small frog *made* a loud noise.

Richard *was awakened* by the noise.

In some sentences the simple predicate is a form of the verb *be*.

Richard *is* my cousin.

Practice: Underline the simple predicate in each sentence.

1. Eduardo painted his grandmother's house.

2. His uncle helped him.

3. The color was chosen by Eduardo's grandmother.

4. The tall trees were trimmed by a neighbor.

Answers to Guide 17 Practice Exercises

Guide 17a

1. no   2. yes   3. no   4. yes

Guide 17b

1. This restaurant has good food.
2. My sister sometimes eats here.

Guide 17c

1. Atlanta is a fast-growing city.
2. It is the capital of Georgia.

Guide 17d

1. Do you know anything about storms?
2. What is a tornado?

Guide 17e

1. Oh no, look at all the cars!
2. What a horrible traffic jam this is!

Guide 17f

1. clouds   2. brothers   3. Susan   4. They

Guide 17g

1. painted   2. helped   3. was chosen
4. were trimmed

The Paragraph

Guide 18a | A paragraph is a group of sentences telling about a single topic or subject.

> Delaware is a small state with a great honor. It was the first state to approve the Constitution of the United States. For this reason it is often called the First State.

Most stories, letters, or reports are divided into paragraphs. The sentences in each paragraph tell about some part of the topic or subject.

Rules for Writing a Paragraph

If the paragraph has a title, use capital letters where they are needed.

Indent the first line of each paragraph and begin other lines at the margin.

Begin the paragraph with a sentence that introduces the topic, or subject.

In other sentences, tell more about the subject.

When something new is told, begin a new paragraph.

Begin each sentence with a capital letter.

Place the right punctuation mark at the end of each sentence.

Make sure to use complete sentences.

Practice: Reread the example paragraph above before writing answers to these questions.

1. What is the topic of the paragraph? _____

2. Which sentence introduces the topic? _____

Guide 18b | Avoid using too many short sentences. Combine several short sentences into one.

> A basketball team has a center. It has two guards. It has two forwards.
> A basketball team has a center, two guards, and two forwards.

Practice: Combine each pair of sentences into one sentence.

1. Lacrosse is played in Canada. It is played in the United States. _____

_____

2. Jorge plays basketball. He plays it every day after school. _____

_____

Philip Wylie was an American writer and he wrote about American life as he saw it and for several years he wrote for a magazine and he also worked on movie scripts. (too many *and*s)

Philip Wylie was an American writer. He wrote about American life as he saw it. For several years he wrote for a magazine. He also worked on movie scripts. (rewritten as separate sentences)

Practice: Rewrite the following long sentence as three separate sentences.

Walt Whitman was a poet and his poems told people about themselves and some of his poems were about the death of Abraham Lincoln. _____

_____

_____

Answers to Guide 18 Practice Exercises

Guide 18a

1. Delaware
2. The first sentence introduces the topic.

Guide 18b

Answers may vary.

1. Lacrosse is played in Canada and the United States.
2. Jorge plays basketball every day after school.

Guide 18c

1. Walt Whitman was a poet. His poems told people about themselves. Some of his poems were about the death of Abraham Lincoln.

Speaking and Listening

Guide 19a Talking with others is called *conversation* or *discussion*. A topic, or subject, is something to talk about.

People take part in a conversation by telling things, by asking questions, and by listening thoughtfully.

Rules for Conversation or Discussion
Stick to the topic being discussed.
Give others an opportunity to talk.
Avoid interrupting others.
Respect the rights and opinions of others.
Ask thoughtful questions.

Rules for Making an Introduction
Pronounce the names of the persons correctly and distinctly.
Tell each person something about the other person, so that he or she may find it easier to make conversation.

> "Trudy, this is Nguyen Duc. He is from Vietnam. Nguyen, this is Trudy Branch. She goes to the same school you do."

Speak the name of an older person first.
Say, "I'm glad to meet you," or something else friendly, when introduced.

Rules for Telephone Conversation
Answer the telephone as soon as possible.
Speak clearly and distinctly into the mouthpiece.
If the call is not for you, say, "Just a minute, please. I'll call . . ."
Let the person who called close the conversation.
Make a call at a time convenient for the other person.
Avoid talking too long.

Rules for Conducting an Interview
Write or telephone for permission and a time to interview the person.
List questions to ask and things to remember.
Make the interview as short as possible.
Thank the person who is interviewed.

Practice: If the statement is true, write *yes.* If it is not true, write *no.*

_____   1. It is all right to interrupt when you have something to say.

_____   2. Let a telephone ring at least four times before you answer it.

_____   3. Make an interview as long as possible to get down all the facts.

Guide 19b When you speak in front of a group, follow these guidelines:

- Speak slowly and clearly enough so that everyone can understand you.

- Make eye contact with the audience.

- Use appropriate language.

- Before you speak, plan the order in which you will say things. When you speak, follow that order.

- Change the volume and tone of your voice to emphasize your main ideas and important points.

- Avoid saying *um*. Try not to use the word *and* too often.

- Finish your talk by repeating your main idea or most important point.

Guide 19c When you listen to a speaker or group of speakers, follow these guidelines:

- Listen carefully and courteously.

- Try to identify a speaker's main ideas.

- Take notes if important information is being presented.

- If the speaker is telling about something that happened, pay attention to the order in which events happened.

- If the speaker is describing something, try to picture it in your mind.

- If the speaker is trying to persuade the audience of something, try to determine which statements are facts and which are opinions.

- Be ready to ask questions when the speaker finishes.

Answers to Guide 19 Practice Exercises

Guide 19a

1. no   2. no   3. no

The Report

Guide 20 Giving a report means telling about something you did, saw, heard, or read. Follow the suggestions given below and those in Guide 18.

- Select a worthwhile topic, or subject, that will interest your listeners.
- Limit the topic to something you can explain fully.
- The topics below are too broad to be explained fully in a report.

  Cities   Africa   Track and Field

The topics below are examples of limited topics that can be used for reports.

  Boston's Subways   Mount Kenya   The World Records of Carl Lewis

- To help select interesting things to tell, think of questions about the topic that you would like to answer.
- Make use of reference books to find information about the topic.
- Begin the report with an interesting sentence that introduces the subject.
- Be sure that every sentence tells something about the topic.
- Tell or write the report in your own words.

Practice: If the statement is true, write *yes*. If it is not true, write *no*.

_____   1. Limit your topic to something you can explain fully.

_____   2. Be sure to include sentences about other topics in your report.

_____   3. Avoid using reference books to find information.

Answers to Guide 20 Practice Exercises

1. yes   2. no   3. no

The Story

Guide 21   A story tells about something that happens to a person or a thing. It is unlike a report in that it may be imaginary. In telling a story, follow the suggestions below and those given in Guide 18.

Character, setting, and plot are the basic parts of all stories. Usually the character is a person. The setting is the time and place where the story happens. Plot is what happens in a story.

- Choose a story that will interest your listeners.
- Look at your listeners.
- Speak distinctly.
- Make the beginning of your story so interesting that the listeners will want to hear the rest of it.
- Describe the character, setting, and plot of your story.
- Tell the important things in the story in the order in which they happened.
- Tell the story with feeling.
- To make the story more interesting, use the exact words of any speakers.
- Use colorful words that tell exactly what you mean to say.
- Avoid overused words: *fine, good, poor, bad, nice, pretty, cute.*
- Try to avoid saying "and-a," "you know," "um," and "like."
- Keep your listeners interested to the end of the story.
- Be sure that your last sentence clearly ends the story.

Practice: If the statement is true, write *yes*. If it is not true, write *no*.

_____   1. A story must always be true rather than imaginary.

_____   2. You should not show any feelings when you tell a story.

_____   3. Your last sentence should let listeners know that the story has ended.

Answers to Guide 21 Practice Exercises

1. no   2. no   3. yes

The Letter
The Friendly Letter

Guide 22a A friendly letter has five parts: the heading, the greeting (or salutation), the body, the complimentary close, and the signature.

(1) The *heading* tells where and when the letter is written.

(2) The *greeting* greets the person to whom the letter is written.

(3) The *body* contains the message.

(4) The *complimentary close* expresses courtesy or affection.

(5) The *signature* is the name of the person writing the letter.

6408 Ellis Avenue
Chicago, IL 60637
January 5, 1998

Dear Barbara,

I have some wonderful news. My sister Susana has been given a scholarship to law school! Isn't that fantastic? No one here can seem to talk about anything else. We're all so happy for her.

I'll bet that you're enjoying your new house. Please send me a picture as soon as you have a chance. From what you said in your last letter, I guess you even like having to mow the lawn.

Everyone here misses you. Write soon.

Your friend,
Victoria

A letter of this kind is called a friendly letter because it is written to a person to show interest and affection. It tells about things of interest to both the writer and the receiver. The lines in the upper right-hand corner are the heading of the letter. *Dear Barbara* is the greeting (or salutation). The lines telling what Victoria has to say make up the body of the letter. The line *Your friend* is the complimentary close. Notice that only the first word in the complimentary close is capitalized. *Victoria* is the signature of the person writing the letter.

Practice: Write the name of each part of a friendly letter given below.

1. Sincerely, _____

2. Dear Mother, _____

3. Jackie _____

Guide 22b Punctuate a friendly letter according to the rules given below.

(1)   In the heading, place a comma between the city and the postal code abbreviation for the state, and between the day of the month and the year. Do not put a period after the postal code abbreviation.

(2)   Place a comma after the greeting.

(3)   Indent each paragraph in the body of the letter.

(4)   Place a comma after the complimentary close.

Practice: On these lines write a heading for a friendly letter. Use your own address and today's date.

1. _____

2. _____

3. _____

Answers to Guide 22 Practice Exercises

Guide 22a
1. Complimentary close
2. Greeting
3. Signature

Guide 22b
Answers will vary.

The Business Letter

Guide 23a A business letter has six parts. In addition to the five parts of the friendly letter, a business letter has an inside address that gives the name and address of the person or company to receive the letter.

> 32 Circle Drive
> Lansing, MN 55950
> February 12, 1999

Titus Worldwide Imports
4140 Doe Run Road
Louisville, KY 40216

Dear Staff:
        Please send me your latest catalog. I am enclosing two dollars in stamps for the postage.

> Very truly yours,
> Godfrey Ingram

Practice: Find the inside address in the example letter and write it on the lines below.

1. _____

2. _____

3. _____

Guide 23b

Punctuate a business letter according to the rules given below.

(1) In the heading, place a comma between the city and the postal code abbreviation for the state, and between the day of the month and the year.

(2) In the inside address, place a period after the person's title, if it is abbreviated, and after each initial. Place a comma between the city and the postal code abbreviation for the state.

(3) Place a colon after the greeting.

(4) Place a comma after the complimentary close.

Practice: If the statement is true, write *yes*. If it is not true, write *no*.

_____ 1. The zip code is part of the inside address.

_____ 2. You should place a comma after the greeting.

_____ 3. You should place a comma after the complimentary close.

Answers to *Guide 23* Practice Exercises

Guide 23a

1. Titus Worldwide Imports
2. 4140 Doe Run Road
3. Louisville, KY 40216

Guide 23b

1. yes   2. no   3. yes

The Envelope Address

Guide 24

Follow the rules below in addressing an envelope.

(1) Place the name of the sender and the complete address in the upper left-hand corner of the envelope.

(2) Place the name and address of the one to receive the letter near the center of the envelope.

(3) In each address, capitalize the name of the person, any title, and the name of the city. Use the postal code abbreviation for the state name. Do not put a period after the postal code abbreviation.

(4) Place a comma between the city and the postal code abbreviation for the state.

Donnie C. Manders
Route 2
Tullahoma, TN 37388

Mrs. Alice Addison
5107 Rainbow Lane
Levittown, PA 19055

Postal Code Abbreviations

Alabama	AL	Kentucky	KY	Ohio	OH
Alaska	AK	Louisiana	LA	Oklahoma	OK
Arizona	AZ	Maine	ME	Oregon	OR
Arkansas	AR	Maryland	MD	Pennsylvania	PA
California	CA	Massachusetts	MA	Puerto Rico	PR
Colorado	CO	Michigan	MI	Rhode Island	RI
Connecticut	CT	Minnesota	MN	South Carolina	SC
Delaware	DE	Mississippi	MS	South Dakota	SD
District of	DC	Missouri	MO	Tennessee	TN
Columbia		Montana	MT	Texas	TX
Florida	FL	Nebraska	NE	Utah	UT
Georgia	GA	Nevada	NV	Vermont	VT
Guam	GU	New Hampshire	NH	Virgin Islands	VI
Hawaii	HI	New Jersey	NJ	Virginia	VA
Idaho	ID	New Mexico	NM	Washington	WA
Illinois	IL	New York	NY	West Virginia	WV
Indiana	IN	North Carolina	NC	Wisconsin	WI
Iowa	IA	North Dakota	ND	Wyoming	WY
Kansas	KS				

Practice: If the statement is true, write *yes*. If it is not true, write *no*.

_____ 1. You should use the correct zip code in every address.

_____ 2. You should write your name in the upper right-hand corner of the envelope.

_____ 3. You should always put a comma between the postal code abbreviation for the state and the zip code.

Answers to Guide 24 Practice Exercises

1. yes   2. no   3. no

Troublesome Words

I and Me

Guide 25a   Use the pronoun *I* as the subject of a sentence. After words of action, such as *see*, *call*, or *meet*, and after such words as *to*, *for*, and *from*, use *me*.

I am now a student council member.

My classmates elected *me* to this position last week.

Almost everyone voted for *me*.

Practice: In these sentences, supply the appropriate form, *I* or *me*.

1. You met _____ last year.

2. _____ played against you in a volleyball game.

Guide 25b   Place the word *I* or *me* last when you speak or write of yourself and others in the same sentence.

She and *I* waited in line.

Marcy, Hamid, and *I* have summer jobs.

Charles asked Beatrix and *me* to join him.

The song was written by Nelson and *me*.

Practice: Rewrite these sentences to show the appropriate use of *I* or *me*.

1. Me and Pat jogged two miles before breakfast. _____

_____

2. Tanya helped I and Alex with the puzzle. _____

_____

Answers to Guide 25 Practice Exercises

Guide 25a

1. me   2. I

Guide 25b

1. Pat and I jogged two miles before breakfast
2. Tanya helped Alex and me with the puzzle.

We and Us

Guide 26   Use the pronoun *we* as the subject of a sentence. Also use such expressions as *we boys* and *we girls* as subjects of sentences. After words of action, such as *gave, saw,* and *teach,* use *us* in place of *we*. Use *us* after such words as *to, for,* and *from* as well.

> *We* work on Saturdays.
>
> It is a way for *us* to make some money.
>
> *We pool guards* teach a lifesaving class.
>
> Many swimmers come to *us experts* for lessons.
>
> A snowstorm caught *us* by surprise.
>
> *We visitors* received a warm welcome.

Practice: In each sentence underline the appropriate word in parentheses.

1. (We, Us) gave a concert.

2. The new play was a treat for (we, us) drama students.

3. (We, Us) theater fans enjoyed the show.

Answers to Guide 26 Practice Exercises

The following words should be underlined:
1. We   2. us   3. We

Himself, Themselves, and Ourselves

Guide 27   Use *himself* (not *hisself*), *themselves* (not *theirselves*), and *ourselves* (not *ourself*).

> The boy saw *himself* in the mirror.
>
> The workers discussed the project among *themselves*.
>
> We had cheered *ourselves* hoarse by halftime.

Practice: In each sentence underline the appropriate word in parentheses.

1. Craig taught (hisself, himself) to play the guitar.

2. The firefighters had earned (themselves, theirselves) a day off.

3. We divided (ourself, ourselves) into two groups.

Answers to Guide 27 Practice Exercises

The following words should be underlined:
1. himself   2. themselves   3. ourselves

Agreement of Verb with Subject

Guide 28a The verbs *is, was, has,* and *does* are used with a sentence subject that names one person or thing. Follow the same rule for *isn't, wasn't, hasn't,* and *doesn't.*

The verbs *are, were, have,* and *do* are used with a subject that names more than one person or thing. Follow the same rule for *aren't, weren't, haven't,* and *don't.*

The *storm is* getting worse.   Some *storms are* dangerous.
Isn't the *wind* blowing hard?   *Don't ships* try to avoid storms?

Study the examples below that show verbs with singular and plural subjects.

Singular	**Plural**
Simon does push-ups.	*Nick and Simon do* push-ups.
Janelle likes archery.	*We* all *like* archery.
She plays tennis well.	*Most* of us *play* tennis.
I play tennis, too.	*Students* at our school *enjoy* sports.
I am not a great player.	*They keep* us fit.

Practice: In each sentence underline the appropriate word in parentheses.

1. Forest fires (has, have) damaged much timberland.

2. (Do, Does) many fires start in the home?

3. People (need, needs) to learn about fire safety.

4. (Don't, Doesn't) it make sense to be careful with fire?

Guide 28b Use *are, were, have,* and *do* with *you.* Use *am, was, have,* and *do* with *I.* Follow the same rule for *aren't, weren't, haven't,* and *don't.*

You are late again today.

Haven't you bought an alarm clock?

I have trouble getting up in the morning.

Don't I always arrive on time?

Practice: In each sentence underline the proper word in parentheses.

1. You (was, were) following me.

2. I (has, have) a question to ask you.

3. (Do, Does) you know the way to the zoo?

> Use *there is, is there, there was,* or *was there* with a subject that names one person or thing. Use *there are, are there, there were,* or *were there* with a subject that names more than one person or thing. Follow the same rule for *isn't, aren't, wasn't,* and *weren't.*

There is a parking space.

There wasn't one a minute ago.

Are there any cars coming?

Weren't there any spaces in front of the store?

Practice: In each sentence underline the proper choice in parentheses.

1. (Was there, Were there) any job openings?

2. (There was, There were) a list in the newspaper.

3. (Isn't there, Aren't there) some jobs listed at the employment agency?

Answers to Guide 28 Practice Exercises

Guide 28a
The following words should be underlined:
1. have   2. Do   3. need   4. Doesn't

Guide 28b
The following words should be underlined:
1. were   2. have   3. Do

Guide 28c
The following words should be underlined:
1. Were there   2. There was   3. Aren't there

A and An

Guide 29 Use the word *an* before a word beginning with a vowel sound. Use the word *a* before a word beginning with a consonant sound.

an avenue	a circle	an insect	a union
a bookcase	an engine	an honor	an umbrella

Practice: In each sentence underline the appropriate word in parentheses.

1. What is (a, an) baker's dozen?

2. It is (a, an) usual way of saying thirteen of something.

3. What (a, an) adventure it was!

The following words should be underlined:
1. a   2. a   3. an

May and Can

Guide 30	Use *may* to ask or give permission to do something. Use *can* to show that you are able to do something.

May we ride the subway today?

Can we get to the stadium on this subway?

Practice: In each sentence underline the appropriate word in parentheses.

1. (May, Can) I look through your telescope?

2. Yes, you (may, can) look through my telescope.

3. (May, Can) you focus it yourself?

The following words should be underlined:
1. May   2. may   3. Can

Teach and Learn

Guide 31	The verb *teach* means "to give instruction or to show how something is done." The verb *learn* means "to receive instruction or to find out how something is done."

Will the instructor *teach* us the backstroke?

Doe *learned* the backstroke easily.

Rather than saying, "She is learning me to dive," say, "She is teaching me to dive." You yourself do the learning. The person who shows you how does the teaching.

Practice: In each sentence underline the appropriate word in parentheses.

1. Who (taught, learned) you to paint?

2. Did your sister (teach, learn) you?

3. I want to (teach, learn) to make pottery.

The following words should be underlined:
1. taught   2. teach   3. learn

Sit and Set

> The verb *sit* means to take a seat or to stay in one place. The verb *set* means to put or place something.

We always *sit* close to the movie screen.

Please *set* the package on the counter.

The three principal parts of these verbs are given below.

sit sat sat   set set set

Practice: In each sentence underline the appropriate word in parentheses.

1. The three of us (sat, set) in the front seat.

2. Donna has (sat, set) the groceries on the table.

3. Lucius has (sat, set) at the same desk for three years.

Answers to Guide 32 Practice Exercises

The following words should be underlined:
1. sat   2. set   3. sat

Word Study
Homophones

Guide 33 Some words are confusing because they sound alike but have different meanings and different spellings. These words are called *homophones*.

ate	We *ate* tacos last night.		hear	Did you *hear* a noise?
eight	*Eight* of us made the team.		here	*Here* I am.
blew	The wind *blew* my hat off.		hour	The play opens in an *hour*.
blue	Some cats have *blue* eyes.		our	*Our* street is paved.
buy	Hal will *buy* a model boat.		its	The dog wagged *its* tail.
by	Tina stood *by* the window.		it's	*It's* nine o'clock.
fair	Was that a *fair* ball?		knot	I can't untie this *knot*.
fare	Have your bus *fare* ready.		not	Howard did *not* go to work.
flower	A rose is a *flower*.		meat	Vegetarians eat no *meat*.
flour	Bread is made with *flour*.		meet	Todd will *meet* us later.
for	I have a telegram *for* you.		new	My *new* watch is broken.
four	We bought *four* tickets.		knew	I *knew* I could do it.
one	A unicycle has *one* wheel.		threw	The goalie *threw* the ball.
won	Shan *won* the poetry prize.		through	We ran *through* the woods.
red	Jacob has *red* hair.		to	Juan drove *to* New Mexico.
read	Have you *read* this book?		too	William saw it, *too*.
right	Turn *right* at the corner.		too	The soup is *too* hot.
write	Did Janis *write* her story?		two	The race is *two* miles long.
road	This *road* is a dead end.		weak	The sick wolf was *weak*.
rode	Hilda *rode* her racing bike.		week	Seven days make a *week*.
sea	The *sea* became rough.		who's	*Who's* at the door?
see	May I *see* your ring?		whose	*Whose* car is that?
their	The trees lost *their* leaves.		your	Don't forget *your* lunch.
there	*There* is no moon tonight.		you're	*You're* ten minutes early.

Practice: In each sentence underline the appropriate word in parentheses.

1. (Whose, Who's) going to be the first (one, won) in the pool?

2. The train (fair, fare) is cheaper if you (buy, by) a round-trip ticket.

3. I've (read, red) that many strange creatures live in the (sea, see).

Answers to Guide 33 Practice Exercises

The following words should be underlined:
1. Who's, one   2. fare, buy   3. read, sea

Synonyms

Words that have the same or nearly the same meanings are called *synonyms.*

above over	jumped leaped	scared frightened
aid help	laughed giggled	shut close
below under	lift raise	shy timid
bright shiny	mistake error	soiled dirty
certain sure	rapidly quickly	yell shout
funny amusing	reply answer	strange odd
huge large	rude impolite	thankful grateful
hurt injured	search hunt	toss throw

Practice: Beside each word below, write its synonym from the example list.

1. certain _____

2. reply _____

3. quickly _____

4. thankful _____

Answers to Guide 34 Practice Exercises

1. sure   2. answer   3. rapidly   4. grateful

Antonyms

| Guide 35 | Words that are opposite in meaning are called *antonyms*. |

absent present	largest smallest	remember forget
against for	least most	rough smooth
fair unfair	leave stay	shortest longest
weak strong	left right	spend save
forward backward	alive dead	begin end
freeze melt	narrow wide	warm cool
honest dishonest	north south	wealthy poor
joy sorrow	pulling pushing	working playing

Practice: Beside each word below, write its antonym from the example list.

1. against _____   3. least   _____

2. joy   _____   4. pushing _____

| Answers to Guide 35 Practice Exercises |

1. for   2. sorrow   3. most   4. pulling

Double Negatives

| Guide 36 | Words such as *no, not, nothing, none, never, hardly,* and *scarcely* are negatives. Two negatives are not needed in the same sentence. |

Avoid two negatives:

Roy *doesn't* want *no* lunch.

He *hasn't never* skipped lunch.

I *can't hardly* understand it.

Use one negative:

Roy *doesn't* want any lunch.

Roy *doesn't* want lunch.

He has *never* skipped lunch.

He *hasn't* ever skipped lunch.

I can *hardly* understand it.

Practice: In each sentence underline the appropriate word in parentheses.

1. Hasn't Janet (never, ever) jumped off the diving board?

2. Carl hadn't heard (none, any) of the facts.

3. I (can, can't) hardly climb any higher.

Answers to Guide 36 Practice Exercises

The following words should be underlined:
1. ever   2. any   3. can

Unnecessary Words

Guide 37	Leave out any word that is not necessary to the meaning of a sentence.

What is the name of this *here* town?

What is the name of this town? (corrected)

Kam *he* lost his job.

Kam lost his job. (corrected)

Yun-hwang and Paul are *like* waiting in line.

Yun-hwang and Paul are waiting in line. (corrected)

Where is my magazine *at*?

Where is my magazine? (corrected)

I have *got* a bad toothache today.

I have a bad toothache today. (corrected)

Practice: Draw a line through the unnecessary words in the sentences below.

1. Jan went and bought a new tennis racket.

2. Kelly, where is your snowboard at?

3. Morris he is like friendly to everyone.

Answers to Guide 37 Practice Exercises

The following words should be marked:
1. went, and   2. at   3. he, like

Expressions to Be Avoided

In speaking and writing in class and at work, avoid expressions that may not be suitable.

Use these expressions:	Avoid these expressions:
am not, is not, are not	ain't
ate	et
bought	buyed
could have	could of
drew, drawn	drawed
grew, grown	growed
heard	heered
knew, known	knowed
must have	must of
ought not	hadn't ought
these people, those people	them people

Practice: In each sentence underline the appropriate word in parentheses.

1. Lester (buyed, bought) a set of snow tires for his car.

2. The other workers (must have, must of) gone home early.

3. (Them, Those) people are from Reno, Nevada.

4. I don't believe he (knowed, knew) the answer.

Answers to Guide 38 Practice Exercises

The following words should be underlined:
1. bought   2. must have   3. Those   4. knew

The Dictionary
Uses of a Dictionary

Use a dictionary to find out the following things about a word: its spelling, its division into syllables, its pronunciation, and its meaning.

The statements given below are true of most dictionaries.

(1)   The entry words are listed in alphabetical order.

(2)   The entry word usually shows how to divide the word into written syllables.

(3)   After the entry word, the word is printed with symbols that show how to pronounce it.

(4)   A key to the meanings of the pronunciation symbols is given at the bottom of the page.

(5)   Entry words are often shown in example sentences or phrases that help make their meanings clear.

Practice: If the statement is true, write *yes.* If it is not true, write *no.*

_____   1. A dictionary shows how to pronounce words.

_____   2. A dictionary gives the meanings of words.

_____   3. Knowing alphabetical order makes it easier to use a dictionary.

Answers to Guide 39 Practice Exercises

The following words should be marked:
1. yes   2. yes   3. yes

Alphabetical Order

Guide 40   **Entry words in a dictionary are listed in alphabetical order so that they can be found more easily. Here are the letters of the alphabet listed in alphabetical order: *a, b, c, d, e, f, g, h, i, j, k, l, m, n, o, p, q, r, s, t, u, v, w, x, y, z.***

aboard	fresh	jockey	ought	unfold
adventure	friend	kneel	puzzle	visit
beehive	government	lawyer	quit	wax
calendar	grape	leather	reason	way
downtown	harbor	medicine	scales	X-ray
elbow	helpful	music	scare	yonder
exact	its	nerve	tease	you've
fountain	itself	ocean	teaspoon	zebra

The words alphabetized above are listed according to the first letter in each one. Notice that when two or more words begin with the same letter, the words are alphabetized according to the second, third, fourth, or fifth letters. In alphabetizing a great many words beginning with the same letter, examine the letters in each word to determine the alphabetical order.

Practice: Write the words on the left in the order in which they would be listed in a dictionary.

mask   cabinet   1. _____   4. _____

country   mast   2. _____   5. _____

fuel   inside   3. _____   6. _____

Answers to Guide 40 Practice Exercises

1. cabinet   3. fuel   5. mask
2. country   4. inside   6. mast

Division of Words

Guide 41   **When it is necessary to divide a word at the end of a line, divide it only at the end of a syllable. Never divide a one-syllable word. Write it all on the next line instead.**

    base (one syllable; not to be divided)

    narrow nar-row (two syllables)

    telephone tel-e-phone (three syllables)

A syllable must have at least one vowel letter—*a, e, i, o,* or *u.* (The letter *y* is sometimes used as a vowel letter, too.) Words of two or more syllables may be divided between like consonant letters, between unlike consonant letters, between vowel letters, between vowel and consonant letters, or between consonant and vowel letters. In writing, place a hyphen (-) at the end of the syllable that ends the line and continue on the next line with the rest of the word. Use a dictionary when you are unsure of how to divide a word.

Practice: Underline each word below that should not be divided in writing.

1. head   4. miner   7. remain   10. woolen

2. down   5. knob   8. fortune   11. flame

3. island   6. yesterday   9. pure   12. gingerbread

Answers to Guide 41 Practice Exercises

The following words should be underlined:
1. head   2. down   5. knob   9. pure   11. flame

Spelling

HANDBOOK

It is important to spell words correctly when you put ideas into written form. The following lists contain words that most people need to be able to spell.

List 1

age	have	most	street	went
bring	head	piece	thank	were
build	heard	please	their	when
care	here	put	then	where
dear	hurt	quite	there	which
does	just	right	these	while
each	knew	said	they	who
find	know	shoes	those	wish
full	learn	since	took	work
half	month	some	want	year

List 2

after	close	guess	order	thought
always	could	heavy	other	through
anything	country	hundred	people	track
beautiful	different	job	ready	truly
business	early	kept	real	until
center	enough	letter	received	usually
chair	every	many	sold	very
change	family	might	spent	whole
chase	felt	money	start	written
chief	friend	never	state	young

PRACTICAL GUIDE TO BETTER ENGLISH   157

INDEX OF HANDBOOK
(The numbers refer to Handbook Guide numbers, not page numbers.)

Abbreviations
    Addresses: 6b, 22, 23, 24
    Days of week: 4
    Initials: 2
    Months of year: 5
    Postal code: 22b, 23b, 24
    Titles with names: 3
Addresses: 6, 24
Alphabetical order: 40
Antonyms: 35
Apostrophes
    Contractions: 13
    Possessives: 15
Articles: 29
Capital letters
    Abbreviations: 2, 3, 4, 5, 6
    Addresses: 6
    Beginning sentences: 1a, 17b
    Days of week: 1h, 4
    Holidays: 1i
    I: 1e
    Initials: 1d, 2
    Letters: 22, 23, 24
    Months of year: 1h, 5
    Persons: 1b
    Pets: 1b
    Places or things: 1f
    Place-name words: 1g
    Quotations: 8
    Titles: 7
    Titles with names: 1c, 3
Commas
    Addresses: 6
    After *yes* and *no*: 11
    Dates: 9
    Direct address: 10
    Letters: 22, 23
    Quotations: 8b, 8c
    Series: 12a
    Two-part sentences: 12b
Composition
    Letters: 22, 23, 24
    Paragraphs: 18
    Reports: 20
    Sentences: 17
    Stories: 21

Contractions: 13
Conversation: 19
Courtesy: 19, 25
Dates: 9
Days of week: 1h, 4
Dictionary
    Alphabetical order: 40
    Dividing words: 41
    Spelling: 42
    Uses: 39
Direct address: 10
Discussion: 19
Double negatives: 36
Homophones: 33
Initials of names: 2
Letter writing
    Addresses: 6, 22, 23, 24
    Envelopes: 24
    Kinds of letters: 22, 23
    Parts of letters: 22, 23
    Titles with names: 3, 23b
    Writing hints: 22, 23
Months of year: 1h, 5
Nouns
    Plural: 14
    Possessive: 15a, 15b
    Singular: 14
Opposites: 35
Paragraphs: 18
Periods
    Addresses: 6
    Abbreviations: 2, 3, 4, 5, 6
    Initials: 2
    Sentences: 17c
    Titles with names: 3
Plural forms of nouns: 14
Possessives: 15
Predicate: 17f, 17g
Pronunciation: 39
Punctuation
    Apostrophes: 13, 15
    Commas: 6, 8b, 8c, 9, 10, 11, 12a, 12b, 22, 23
    Exclamation points: 17e
    Periods: 2, 3, 4, 5, 6, 17c
    Question marks: 17d

Quotation marks: 7b, 8
Quotations: 8
Sentences
    Avoiding too many *and*s: 18c
    Capitalization: 1a, 17b
    Combining: 12b, 18b
    End punctuation: 17c–e
    Predicate: 17f, 17g
    Questions: 17d
    Statements: 17c
    Subject: 17f
    Two-part: 12b
Singular and plural forms of nouns: 14
Speaking and listening: 19, 20, 21
Spelling: 42
Subject of a sentence: 17f
Subject-verb agreement: 28
Titles: 7
Titles with names: 1c, 3
Verbs
    Agreement with subject: 28
    Ate, eaten: 16
    Became, become: 16
    Began, begun: 16
    Blew, blown: 16
    Bring, brought: 16
    Broke, broken: 16
    Came, come: 16
    Did, done: 16
    Don't, doesn't: 28
    Drank, drunk: 16
    Drove, driven: 16
    Fell, fallen: 16
    Flew, flown: 16
    Froze, frozen: 16
    Gave, given: 16
    Grew, grown: 16
    Has, have: 28
    Helping verbs: 16
    Is, are: 28
    Knew, known: 16
    Learn, learned: 16
    May, can: 30

HANDBOOK

Principal parts: 16
Ran, run: 16
Rang, rung: 16
Rode, ridden: 16
Rose, risen: 16
Sang, sung: 16
Sank, sunk: 16
Sat, set: 16, 32
Saw, seen: 16
Spoke, spoken: 16
Swam, swum: 16
Swing, swung: 16
Teach, taught: 16, 31
There is, there are: 28
Threw, thrown: 16
Took, taken: 16
Was, were: 28
Went, gone: 16
Wrote, written: 16

Word study
  a, an: 29
  Alphabetical order: 40
  Antonyms: 35
  Contractions: 13
  Don't, doesn't: 28
  Double negatives: 36
  Expressions to be avoided: 38
  Has, have: 28
  Helping verbs: 16
  Himself, themselves, ourselves: 27
  Homophones: 33
  I, me: 25
  Is, are: 28
  May, can: 30
  Negatives: 36
  Pronunciation: 39

Sit, sat, set: 32
Synonyms: 34
Teach, learn: 31
There is, there are: 28
To, two, too: 33
Unnecessary words: 37
Using *I*: 25
Verb forms: 16
Vocabulary: 33, 34, 35
Was, were: 28
We, us: 26
Words of opposite meaning: 35
Words that mean the same: 34

Score Chart

LESSON	PERFECT SCORE	MY SCORE	LESSON	PERFECT SCORE	MY SCORE	LESSON	PERFECT SCORE	MY SCORE
1	48		34	28		67	20	
2	36		35	28		68	23	
3	34		36	30		69	22	
4	16		37	25		70	30	
5	78		38	20		71	26	
6	20		39	21		72	19	
7	24		40	18		73	26	
8	17		41	84		74	36	
9	16		42	27		75	28	
11	28		44	40		77	28	
12	45		45	19		78	75	
13	18		46	44		79	70	
14	48		47	30		80	21	
15	67		48	24		81	22	
16	18		49	18		82	9	
17	49		50	28		83	38	
18	21		51	26		84	20	
19	30		52	24		85	22	
20	27		53	24		86	35	
22	35		55	50		88	30	
23	36		56	47		89	22	
24	34		57	40		90	33	
25	19		58	20		91	35	
26	19		59	18		92	86	
27	19		60	16		93	30	
28	17		61	20		94	46	
29	36		62	60		95	44	
30	36		63	30		96	36	
31	30		64	40		97	40	
33	40		66	24		98	84	